THAT'S RACIST!

How the Regulation of Speech and Thought Divides Us All

ADRIAN HART

SOCIETAS
essays in political
& cultural criticism

imprint-academic.com

Published in the UK by
Imprint Academic, PO Box 200, Exeter EX5 5YX, UK

Distributed in the USA by
Ingram Book Company,
One Ingram Blvd., La Vergne, TN 37086, USA

ISBN 9781845407551

A CIP catalogue record for this book is available from the
British Library and US Library of Congress

Cover design by Andrew Smith:
www.behance.net/andyartdirector

Contents

Acknowledgements

I'm guessing most books are the result of collective efforts, and this one is no exception. *That's Racist!* attempts to expand on ideas and arguments first developed with *The Manifesto Club* (www.manifestoclub.com) which campaigns against hyper-regulation in everyday life. I am particularly indebted to Manifesto Club director Josie Appleton for her support and encouragement, and also to the bank of ideas built up over the years by the online current affairs magazine *spiked*.

The campaigns by East London Workers Against Racism (ELWAR) in the 1980s were my formative inspiration. There is no space to mention everyone from back then, but I cannot go without acknowledging the contribution made by Nigel Lewis, Keith Tompson, and especially Kenan Malik, to working through the challenges posed by both racism and anti-racism.

In getting this book off the ground, heartfelt thanks are due to Rob Lyons, Andy Duck, Lesley Katon, Tim Rich and River Sweeney. Along the way, discussion and encouragement from Shirley Lawes, Daniel Ben-Ami, James Heartfield and Kevin Rooney were vital. But throughout the process of getting these ideas untangled and on paper, there was Jennie Bristow (whom I can't thank enough). Not least, I couldn't have written this book without the support and unending patience of Julia Basnett.

Introduction

It's Monday morning and another workshop in another school. This time the school, in Essex, has quite a few black children and, the council tell us, racist incidents occur regularly. Seated in front of the video camera is a 10-year-old black boy: we'll call him Joe. Apparently, Joe has been the victim of a number of incidents officially recorded by the school as part of its race equality duties. Before we start I ask Joe if he thinks there is racism in his school. 'No,' he says, 'this is a good school.' 'But we heard mention of some problems… things that happened to you?' I say. Joe looks thoughtful, then smiles. 'Well, some children say things but I say sticks and stones — you know what I mean?'

I like Joe. He seems older than his years, very funny and very confident. He isn't finished: 'You know, it doesn't matter, the colour of your skin. It's what's on the inside that counts.'

Later, as the break-time bell rings, Joe darts off to join his friends in the playground. The two young drama tutors in charge of the anti-racism day discuss Joe's reluctance to acknowledge his experience of racism. As I listen to my colleagues talk I look out of the classroom window. There must be a hundred or more children in the playground. This interests me because it's their world — if I could have my way, the anti-racism video that I have been hired to make for the council would be filmed out there, rather than in workshops. Joe has joined a group of friends and they're all leaping around, wide-eyed as though they had just heard the entire Arsenal team were visiting the school. They mob-wrestle each other and collapse to the ground giggling. Suddenly they leap up and disperse in all directions.

I look for Joe. He's now at the far end of the playground. How did he get there so fast? Now huddled with a completely different group of boys, Joe has produced a set of football cards. My drama tutor colleagues are wondering if Joe is either 'in denial' of racist bullying or just too frightened to speak up.

I think it was this moment that triggered the questions. The first was 'Does this school *really* have a problem with racism?' The teachers were unanimous on that one—'absolutely not'. They were adamant that this was a lovely school and assumed I knew that the council required them to identify and report 'all manifestations of racism, however trivial they may seem'. I had been naive about the purpose of 'racist incident reporting'. But it was the contrast between the exuberant playground of children and the 'racism awareness' drama workshops they were about to attend that prompted the second question: *What the hell were we doing here?*

I wrote these paragraphs back in 2007. The Essex primary schools project, titled *Watch out for Racism!*, had run for most of the previous year. By the time it ended, all I wanted to do was to put my camera away and research, write and make sense of the disquieting phenomenon I had observed.

It was bad enough that teachers had felt obliged to record anything and everything that might be perceived as a racist incident. One head teacher later told me how awkward it was handling incidents involving six- and seven-year-olds: 'The child concerned hasn't made any complaint at all, but one of my staff has felt that there's been an element of racism. We've had a few where the children are best friends and so the trick is to try and handle the thing without it breaking up the friendship or instilling the idea of racism when really they haven't any idea what that is.'

But even our workshops, explicitly designed to explain race issues, brimmed with the potential to confuse and divide. Why, when the children were inventing their own intrinsically anti-racist playground community, were they required to ponder the importance of 'race' and 'identity'? Those early questions began a process which led to the publication, in 2009, of *The Myth of Racist Kids: Anti-Racist Policy and the Regulation of School Life*.[1]

By then, I had made some sense of the Essex project. At the beginning of 2006, when I was hired as the project's filmmaker, both myself and my drama tutor colleagues had been informed we were to visit four schools experiencing 'problems' in relation to their pupils and 'incidents'. As the project brief had passed from Essex council to the London-based young people's theatre that was to deliver it, the idea that the county's schools were in express need of an anti-racism intervention was simply presumed.

For me, the project was immediately at odds with the reality we encountered in these schools. Relatively large numbers of kids from black, Asian and mixed backgrounds merged and, unsurprisingly, they played happily with the majority. It seemed to me that these schools were not experiencing problems: they were simply carrying out a government requirement to record 'racist incidents'. For the teachers, the fact that the children would sometimes fall out and pick on each other's differences was entirely unremarkable.

Yet for Essex council, there certainly was 'a problem' – in that schools were not recording incidents enough. When I unearthed council documentation from its website, the impetus for launching anti-racist interventions became clearer.[2] The council's assessment of the previous three years' 'racist incident' figures was that too few schools were submitting data; in many cases none at all. In response to this, it proposed letters to 'under-reporting' schools, pointing out that 'high levels of reported incidents are the result of good practice rather than the converse'. Compliant schools, noted the council approvingly, were using 'zero tolerance' policies to generate the desired figures. These were the schools to which we had been sent, where it had been understood that incidents must be recorded 'however trivial they may seem'.

'You can't win this one', said one despairing head teacher. 'If you don't report incidents you're told you're not being aware of racism; if you do report it, there'll be someone who decides there's a major problem in the school.' Eager to assist in my research, another Essex head sent me a selection of incident forms. A typical incident in her school was a playground spat in which 'child A' had called 'child B' a 'chocolate bar' or 'white trash'.

However, the council had another problem. The zero tolerance dragnet was proving itself most effective amongst nine- to 11-year-olds: arguably an age group for whom 'inappropriate' banter and insult exchange and mistaken use of adult terms is standard practice. And so it seemed the council wanted to tick two boxes at once: it wanted schools to report *more* incidents and thereby demonstrate their vigilance, *and* it felt obliged to show it was doing something to counter racism among nine- to 11-year-olds.

One solution, apparently, was our project. Alongside staff training and racism awareness components within Personal, Social and Health Education (PSHE) and Citizenship classes, one further 'action to be taken' was *Watch out for Racism!* By commissioning this project Essex hoped 'to help schools address issues of racism in/with pupils' and remind teachers of their responsibilities in 'responding to racist incidents'. To this end, it was proposed that the project's DVD and educational pack would be distributed to all of Essex's primary schools as a Key Stage 2 educational resource.

Making sense of the Essex project was, therefore, something of a 'catch-up' moment for me. It was the moment when I realised that schools were becoming shackled to a divisive and cynical policy that, once implemented, produced statistics that triggered 'actions' that, in turn, produced more statistics. As the figures for racist incidents began to grow, so too did the assumption that they indicated a pressing crisis of serious racist bullying amongst children. By 2007, *Channel 4 News* was reporting a figure of 95,000 officially-recorded racist incidents that it had gathered from just 90 local authorities, accounting for the four years since reporting had begun in 2002/3. An expert told Channel 4 that the figures were merely 'the tip of the iceberg'.[3]

The aim of this book is to explain how it is anti-racist policy, rather than racism, that is driving these statistics. I argue that, far from being a society in the grip of racism, Britain in 2014 is — like the playground at Joe's school in Essex — a place where people of different ethnic origins are generally at ease with one another. In Chapter 1, I recount my memories of anti-racist campaigning in the 1980s, which contrast vividly with the way that things are now. Yet as everyday racism has diminished, there has been an explosion in anti-racist policies, which emphasise differences, inflame tensions and create divisions. In exploring this paradox, I reflect on the changing meaning of both racism and anti-racism over the past couple of decades, and some examples of the mess caused by policies designed to enforce 'tolerance' by monitoring people's speech and thoughts.

Anti-racist policy

In discussing the form taken by anti-racist policy today and the incredible grip it holds on schools, workplaces and public institutions, this book pays a great deal of attention to the 1999 Macpherson Report and the amended race relations legislation that it inspired. The Macpherson Report resulted from an official inquiry in 1998, chaired by Sir William Macpherson, which examined the events surrounding the murder of the black teenager Stephen Lawrence, including the botched police investigation into this crime. In his report, Macpherson moved significantly beyond issues directly relating to the murder. He concluded that the 'corrosive disease' of racism, evident within institutions such as the police, was a society-wide problem. Moreover, it was a problem that persisted in all public institutions because of a failure 'to recognise and address its existence and causes by policy, example and leadership'.[4]

Underpinned by legal duties imposed via the Race Relations (Amendment) Act 2000, a plethora of official anti-racist policy embraced Macpherson's view, and very often quoted directly from it. In local authority guidance for schools, the definition of a racist incident was invariably the one recommended by Macpherson: *'any incident perceived to be racist by the victim or any other person.'* And for a new, Macpherson-inspired generation of anti-racism officials, there was nothing perverse in encouraging schools to generate increasing numbers of 'racist incidents': this was seen as part and parcel of exposing society's corrosive disease.

Importantly, to be seen as fully engaged in such an example-setting practice was one way schools and local authorities could defend themselves from the accusation that they too were institutionally racist. 'Failure to investigate even where an incident appears to be of a relatively minor nature', warned government guidance, 'could be seen as condoning racism and could be used as evidence that a school is not taking seriously its legal duties under the Race Relations (Amendment) Act.'[5]

Capturing the attention of the education sector, Macpherson had said: 'how society rids itself of [racist] attitudes is not something we can prescribe, except to stress the need for education and example at the youngest age, and an overall attitude of "zero tolerance" of racism within our society.'[6] The phrase 'zero tolerance' would appear countless times in public sector equalities policy statements and guidance. And for the anti-racists now focusing their attention on children, 'nip it in the bud' became a phrase I would read and hear time and again.

Underpinning this fantasy—that speech regulation and awareness-raising workshops can remove racism before it flowers—is the assumption that children are conditioned, from birth, by the persistent racism of their parents' generation. In this sense, a playground 'racist' insult is perceived as the tip of a hidden iceberg of endemic playground racism which, in turn, becomes the tip of a hidden iceberg of parent-world racism, extending across society at large.

In the years following the publication of *The Myth of Racist Kids*, I have been struck by the extent to which the adult world has become submerged by the same prejudice. The reality gap between increasingly diverse playgrounds of children, at ease with themselves and each other, and the handwringing of anti-racist officialdom now reveals itself way beyond the school gate. As prejudice and discrimination continue to ebb away, as ethnic diversity continues to flourish in unprecedented ways, a new-look anti-racism, seemingly obsessed with correct or incorrect language and behaviour, is on the rise. The febrile atmosphere that has engulfed British Premier League football, discussed in the final chapter of this book, is one example; the obsession with 'diversity training', discussed in Chapter 3, is another. Many of us will have experienced, witnessed or heard of examples of this censorious trend in our everyday lives.

Why is this so? It is true that unpleasant instances of explicit racism still occasionally occur but when they do we are shocked precisely because they are an oddity. They feel like they belong to the past. Yet such occurrences are eagerly seized upon and described as 'the tip of the iceberg'.[7] The phrase chimes perfectly with the Macpherson worldview because, through appeals to the *hidden* and the *unwitting*, it evokes the idea of a rump of racism far larger than any tangible evidence can easily reveal.

The phrase assures us that whatever evidence we can find, it is nothing compared to the vast, perilous reality we have yet to find. In many cases 'the tip' reveals no hard evidence of racism at all. But that doesn't matter to this way of thinking — whatever constitutes 'the tip' (a person's incorrect words or opinions, their conduct, a set of statistics derived from schools) is merely perceived as proof of its cause.

This book argues that the fantasy racism targeted by society's post-Macpherson thinking is *the racism of the past*. Worse, the adoption of this mindset by the political and media elite has led, first, to policies that actively create and exacerbate divisions and, second, to the fostering of a culture of conformism that stifles our ability to speak, act and even think freely. The manner in which today's anti-racism encourages racial etiquette and a narrow focus on visible differences does nothing to address social inequality or, indeed, the many other social problems we face. Rather, it gifts the political elite with the 'divide and rule' service not far different to that which was once provided by racism. 'There is no better way of heading off the nightmare of unified political action by the economically disadvantaged', noted the late, left-wing philosopher Brian Barry, '…than to set different groups of the disadvantaged against one another.'[8]

In this respect, anti-racist policy assists in the task of emotional governance,[9] placing a check on our public actions and private thoughts. The democratic ideal of being permitted to speak freely, but also to listen freely and decide for ourselves between right and wrong, finds itself on the back foot. Meanwhile, pledging allegiance to 'zero tolerance' policies, loudly condemning 'racist' or 'racially offensive' words and phrases or 'insensitive' criticism (while choosing only correct, inoffensive language for yourself) and keeping constant vigil for evidence of racism has become mandatory if you want to get ahead in public life.

'Racial Correctness' is, perhaps, the best description for this self-aggrandising, finger-pointing, yet somewhat fear-driven demeanour. Its power is evident in the fact that, while people will privately confess their misgivings about some of the consequences of the censorious and divisive policies that masquerade as attempts to support 'diversity', few dare voice their concerns publicly, for fear of attracting that reputation-damaging, often career-ending response, 'That's racist!'

This book is an attempt to tackle openly some of the concerns about the trajectory of the new anti-racism, and the consequences of its policies for schools, workplaces and public institutions. My hope is that it will inspire a more honest reflection on the meaning of racism and anti-racism in Britain today, and a debate about the kind of codes and policies that have developed over the past few years.

Endnotes:

1   Hart, A. (2009) *The Myth of Racist Kids: Anti-Racist Policy and the Regulation of School Life,* London: The Manifesto Club. Accessed 05 June 2014. Available at: http://www.manifestoclub.com/

mythracistkids

2   Scott, A. (2006) 'Promoting race equality', Part 1 Report, Scrutiny Panel of the Children, Young People and Schools Policy Development Group, 5 April. Accessed 21 May 2014. Available at: http:// tinyurl.com/pcy62d7

3   See: *Channel 4 News* (2007) 'Racism in Schools', 24 May. Accessed 05 June 2014. Available at: http://www.channel4.com/news/articles/ society/education/revealed+racism+in+schools/529297.html

4   Macpherson, W. (1999) *The Stephen Lawrence Inquiry*, UK Government Command Paper 4262–1, p28. Accessed 21 May 2014. Available at: https://www.gov.uk/government/publications/the-stephen-lawrence-inquiry

5   See: *Bullying Around Racism, Religion and Culture* (2006), Department for Education and Skills, p48. Accessed 05 June 2014. Available at: http://www.insted.co.uk/racist-bullying-april11.pdf

6   Macpherson, W. (1999) *Op. cit.,* Ch 7.42.

7   For a most recent example see: Talwar, D. (2012) 'More than 87,000 racist incidents recorded in schools', *BBC News Online*, 23 May: 'Sarah Soyei, of the anti-racism educational charity, Show Racism the Red Card (SRRC), said: "Unfortunately, the numbers of recorded racist incidents are just the tip of the iceberg".' Accessed 21 May 2014. Available at: http://www.bbc.co.uk/news/education-18155255

8   Barry, B. (2001) *Culture & Equality*, Cambridge: Polity Press, pp11–12.

9   For a useful discussion on 'emotional governance' see: Kyriakides, C., and Torres, R. (2012) *Race Defaced: Paradigms of Pessimism, Politics of Possibility,* Stanford, California: Stanford University Press.

Chapter One

Racism in Britain: Reality and Illusion

If I were to pick out one overriding reason why Britain's increasingly 'mixed-race', mixed-cultured and ever-expanding ethnic diversity is a wholly good thing, it would be the contribution this has made to the evaporation of racial prejudice and intolerance. The more we interact with the social diversity around us, the more we establish common human bonds and the less racist we become. Contrary to the picture painted by the new anti-racism it is the *rarity* of ethnic tension and violence today that makes it so shocking to us, and anti-racism itself that keeps racial sensitivities stirring.

A study of 13 years of data from the *British Social Attitudes* (BSA) survey[1] revealed a sudden and pronounced decline in racial prejudice from the end of the 1980s and onwards into the next decade. It concluded that with every generation born after the period of mass black and Asian immigration there came another seismic drop in levels of prejudice. In 2010, a study of all-white juries[2] failed to reveal any evidence at all of jury discrimination when comparing cases involving white and non-white defendants.

Changes in attitudes reflect changes in people's experience of living with, working alongside and loving people from different ethnic groups to their own. In twenty-first-century Britain, the extent of white/non-white intermarriage and pro-creation is unprecedented, and this trend is continuing.[3] Not surprising then, that the age-old distaste for 'mixed-race' marriage is dying out with the generations that held these attitudes.[4]

Formed by the circumstances of yesterday's world, the racialised attitudes of these older generations are regarded by younger people as archaic. Reflecting on the 'race-talk' of adults, one 14-year-old Bangladeshi girl told the Runnymede Trust: 'We're kids, we're growing up… they're always judging us… I think the older generation just, really, need to be quiet!'[5] Trevor Phillips, former chair of the Equality and Human Rights Commission (EHRC), put it well when he said, 'the trend is clear: the younger you are, the less prejudiced you are'.[6]

But if racist attitudes are generational, so too are many of the anti-racist ideas and arguments we hear today. Ideologically moulded in decades when racism *was* everyday and endemic, the hand-wringing over what is or might be racist is increasingly regarded by young people as insensitively out of touch. Yet an anti-racist outlook rooted in times gone by has had a disproportionate effect on the regulation of British society in the present. While the mood of our times is elevated by youthful enthusiasm for an unfolding cosmopolitan diversity, this mood is haunted by the suspicion that racial intolerance continues to lurk within all of us, only waiting for an excuse to explode outwards.

For most of us, regardless of our ethnicity, our day-to-day experience of society is likely to be devoid of evidence of racism. Yet, few of us feel we can draw much significance from this experience — we worry that racism must be simply happening somewhere else, to someone else. Racism, it is said, must have gone 'underground'; it is 'covert', hiding under the surface and inside *ourselves*. This assumption, of ubiquitous and *unwitting* racism, was the conclusion reached by the Macpherson Report on the inquiry into the murder of Stephen Lawrence, and promoted by campaigners and politicians subsequently.

Racism in Britain: then and now

The rise of racism as a socio-political force is a relatively modern historical phenomenon emerging in parallel with the imperialist conquests and rivalries of Britain and other western powers. From the late nineteenth century and for most of the twentieth, the 'race card' was played again and again by the British elite as a way of dividing its white and immigrant working class, or of rallying national support for (white) 'Britain' against 'the rest'. This divisive strategy worked: while millions in the 1820s had signed petitions demanding an end to slavery, by 1920 anti-black racism had exploded into violence in the ports of Cardiff and Liverpool.[7]

But it was only after the Second World War that Britain became worthy of the epithet 'a racist society'. Mass immigration from former British colonies provided a visible focus for smouldering racist attitudes to re-ignite and transform into the popular racism that was to last for decades. Events such as the 1958 Notting Hill riots triggered fears of growing disorder and helped initiate the 1965 Race Relations Act. The Act outlawed discrimination on the grounds of 'colour, race, or ethnic or national origins' in public places. It therefore became unlawful to refuse access to public places (hotels, restaurants, pubs, cinemas or public transport), or to refuse to rent out accommodation, on the grounds of race. Stirring up racial hatred ('incitement') also became a criminal offence.

For the past 30 years, the political ideology of racism has receded dramatically. The comparison between Britain in, say, 1964 and the social landscape 50 years on could not be more dramatic. Today, for example, it is impossible to imagine a mainstream political party approving placards with the slogan 'If you want a nigger for a neighbour vote Labour'. Indeed, attempts to stoke or exploit ethnic tension will typically backfire in no uncertain terms: as indicated by the furore over the anti-EU propaganda put out by the UK Independence Party (Ukip).[8] While individual prejudices persist, they are rarely confidently expressed, and associated with older generations or those on the fringes of mainstream politics.

Crucially, racial prejudices have become unplugged from any systematic pattern or official sanction. In the past couple of decades, the racist ideologies promoted by the elite, which once gave individual prejudice a steady green flashing light, have been replaced by an equally purposeful anti-racism, born of the desire to maintain racial order.[9] This new anti-racism takes the form of policies that promote regulation of social behaviour and attitudes in the name of multiculturalism and the management of 'diversity'.

Laws restricting immigration remain intact, and we continue to hear periodic tirades from politicians and newspapers against immigrants, refugees and asylum seekers. But this does not alter the reality that twenty-first-century Britain is more diverse and more tolerant than ever before. British-born generations of black and Asian citizens have been a significant driver for this change. Especially in cities, ethnicity is not an issue in most people's everyday lives.

The fact that Britain's largest (and exponentially increasing) minority group is the category formerly known as 'mixed race' ought to tell us something about the scale of ethnic fusion. As noted above, 'mixed' marriages have become so normal that most people do not notice them at all and, on an everyday level, people mix, collaborate, date, cohabit and make friends with other people from every background. Just look at any local primary or secondary school, in cities whether in the North or South of England: the crucible they provide for living out diversity plays a key role in forging cooperation and shared perspectives.

The evidence, then, seems scarcely to bear out the idea of 'racist Britain'. Yet this idea continues to persist. One revealing analysis of the Home Office Citizenship Survey 2010/11 states that '44 percent of people in England and Wales thought that there was more racial prejudice than five years ago' – but it also notes, 'White people were more likely to think that levels of racial prejudice had increased than people from ethnic minority backgrounds (47% compared with 23%)'.[10] Most black and minority ethnic people do *not* consider they would be treated worse by any of the five criminal justice agencies or any of the eight public service organisations.[11]

The fact that white British people are so much more likely than those from minority ethnic groups to agree with the proposition that we live in a more racist society than ever indicates that increasing sensitivity to race and to racism has little to do with the day-to-day lives of those people who would be targeted by racial prejudice.

Chapter 3 will examine how this belief, that Britain is a society where racial prejudice is endemic, became institutionalised via the 1998 Macpherson Report, the inquiry that led to it and the consequences that followed: a process that I shall refer to simply as 'Macpherson'. From Macpherson flowed magnified fears about underestimating racism, seeming insensitive to its victims and being unmasked as 'a little bit racist' (or just woefully ignorant). These were the anxieties that would be driven along by the new industry of 'official' anti-racism.

However, the proponents of the new anti-racism are singularly influenced by the ghosts of racism past – the ideas, attitudes and actions that characterised the post-war decades and reached their peak in the 1980s. As a result, today's anti-racist outlook constantly imagines the lurking presence of an everyday popular racism which we might better describe as a spectre of racism etched by recent history. By emphasising the dangers posed by 'unwitting' thought processes, Macpherson supplied traction to the idea that the racism of the past has not gone away, but rather hidden itself 'underground'. From then on, an anti-racist radar has scanned for the signs of a phantom 'fifth column', a zombie-racism rising up from its sleep.

The tools developed for slaying the menace of zombie racism are those that befit the 'signs' – *a zero tolerance approach* to all moments of untamed hate speech and the cultivation of social conformity over what is or is not the correct way to speak or think about race. It is argued that we should not be tricked by the illusions that flow from images of positive, hopeful, transrace futures. The exemplars of the new anti-racism advise caution in the face of surface reality, alerting us to the sinister reality of what lies beneath. 'London's Olympic summer', commented the race equality think-tank the Runnymede Trust early in 2013, 'projected an image of a nation at ease with itself, united in diversity. And yet a slew of incidents in recent months on the football field, twitter and beyond revealed *a more sinister picture…*' (my emphasis).[12]

In fact, it seems that the 'more sinister picture' of racist Britain that forms the backdrop to such concerns lies not in anything that happens in the here and now, but rather in the recent history of the 1980s. If we think back to British society less than 30 years ago, we can understand why racism so horrifies those of us who believe in a tolerant, equal society, and why campaigners today are so sensitive to apparent manifestations of such prejudice. The trouble is that, by reacting to isolated or presumed expressions of prejudice today as though they prove the persistence of the problems of the past, the new anti-racism both trivialises the experience of ethnic minority groups living through genuinely racist times, and blows current manifestations of 'racism' out of all proportion.

Eighties Britain: a truly racist place to be

Allow me to take you on a brief trip down my own memory lane, to March 1990. East London Workers Against Racism (ELWAR) was meeting, as usual, in the back room of a Bethnal Green community centre. Nigel was in charge, surrounded by the usual crew of committed campaigners, and a couple of new joiners, including me. As we waited for nightfall, we rolled up hundreds of posters and mixed up tubs of wallpaper paste. The posters proclaimed 'Defend the Stepney Four!', and were part of our campaign to bolster support for Bengali teenagers Malik Miah, Abdul Alim and two others. All four had been arrested and charged with attempted murder following the stabbing of a white man.

The run-up to these arrests provides important context. Throughout the 1980s, the east London borough of Tower Hamlets had witnessed a steady stream of violent racist attacks against Bengalis. The police were indifferent and ineffectual. Not surprising, then, that a new generation of Asian youth began to organise themselves to fight back. For many young

Bengali men and boys, it felt like they had no choice but to defend their homes — their mothers, fathers and sisters. 'The police ignore our calls for help', said one youth in an interview for the Workers Against Racism newsletter, 'so we have to defend our families ourselves. Even when the police do come, they always blame us for starting the trouble.'

A few years earlier, Malik Miah's father, Waris Ali, had been beaten up by a white gang carrying iron bars — they stamped on his leg to break it. His mother, Sara Bibi, was attacked by a gang who beat her around the head with a piece of wood embedded with nails. His brother, Mukith, was attacked with a Stanley knife and cut down the entire length of his back. 'They tried to sacrifice him', recalled Mac Miah, another brother.[13]

In February 1990, a 17-year-old white student, John Stoner, was stabbed at Morpeth School in Globe Town. Asian students were implicated. The school had, by this time, become a tinder-box of resentment. Two years earlier Bengali students had staged a strike in protest against racist harassment by fellow white students, and local white resentment toward Bengali youth was also building up. The stabbing immediately resulted in an angry demonstration outside Bethnal Green police station calling for an inquiry into Bengali violence against whites. After the demonstration white youths, including stewards from the protest, drove a car around Stepney hurling racist abuse. They stopped and attacked a group of Bengalis; in the midst of the fray, one of the racists was stabbed. The police arrested Malik Miah and his friends near the scene. 'We have been attacked for years and the police have done nothing', said Sara Bibi. 'Now one white man gets stabbed and the police arrest these boys for attempted murder, something they had nothing to do with.'[14]

The Stepney Four campaign was about defending all Bengali youth in Tower Hamlets and highlighting the police's criminalisation strategy against them. In the 1980s, ELWAR had something of a reputation, summed up by one of its slogans 'fighting racism: *it's up to us*'. It took direct action by organising street patrols and protecting the homes of families under siege.

The writer and broadcaster Kenan Malik recalls spending most of 1984 as an ELWAR activist camped out in the home of one such family. Malik, who is highly critical of today's jaundiced anti-racist outlook, reinforces the point that racism in the 1970s and 80s was 'vicious, visceral and often fatal'.[15] It was a racism that grew virulent as a consequence of the indifference, if not direct participation, of the police. It was also a consequence of the tacit approval of racism evident in the everyday actions of magistrates, politicians and immigration officers. This is the 'sinister picture' imprinted on my memory, and it bears no comparison with today.

We can go back a bit further, to 1981 — a particularly bad year. It began with the now-notorious New Cross fire, which killed 13 young black party-goers after an arson attack. The police dismissed the possibility of a racist motive despite a wave of attacks in the locality. Chanting 'Thirteen dead, Nothing said', 15,000 black Londoners marched in protest. Across April and March, tensions continued to build in direct response to racist attacks but also to the police assault, dubbed 'Operation Swamp 81'. In Brixton, south London, 120 plain clothed officers stopped and searched 943 people in just six days, arresting 118. Riots broke out in St Paul's in Bristol and soon after in Brixton. These riots — some of the worst Britain had ever seen — shook the political elite, and the government quickly announced the appointment of Lord Scarman to conduct an inquiry. The first 'Minister for Race Relations', George Young, was appointed.

As the Scarman Inquiry opened on 15 June, murderous racist attacks continued. A disabled Sikh woman was killed in a firebomb attack on her home in Leeds and, in Leamington Spa, an elderly Asian woman was set alight after racists doused her in petrol.[16] Another firebombing took place in Walthamstow, north-east London. In the early hours of 2 July 1981, Parveen Khan and her three children burned to death after petrol was sprayed through the letter-box; her husband survived, but was seriously burned. The inquest recorded a verdict of unlawful killing but took no interest in claims that this had been a racist attack.[17]

Fresh riots in Brixton were accompanied by disturbances across London. Britain's cities erupted: in Liverpool, Birmingham, Leeds, Leicester, Sheffield, Portsmouth, Preston, Newcastle, Derby, Southampton, Nottingham, Bedford, Edinburgh, Wolverhampton, Stockport, Blackburn, Huddersfield, Reading, Chester and Aldershot. On 25 November 1981, Lord Scarman's report was published.[18] It explicitly rejected the idea that systematic racism lay behind the riots but, in a coded form, accepted 'complex political, social and economic factors' as culpable.

If there was one overriding conclusion to the Scarman Report, it was the linking of volatile race relations with a recognition that the state needed to act urgently to improve racial disadvantage. Black citizens, stated Scarman, must be assisted in gaining a greater stake in society. In 1981 also, the interim Rampton Report[19] (a forerunner of the Swann Report) into the education of children from ethnic minority groups was published, concluding that poor attainment was the product of low expectations and racism among white teachers and society as a whole.

The birth and growth of official anti-racism

The call for action made by Scarman and Rampton did not sit well with the Tory elite. However, given the vexed question of racial discord had implicated Britain's major cities, the race relations challenge was enthusiastically taken up by the Labour-controlled local authorities. These authorities were fast developing a radical reputation, encapsulated in the 'loony left' label applied by the Conservative government and the right-leaning press. The need to quell black urban rebellion ensured that the Conservative government funded those urban local authorities in the front line, via the Urban Programme initiative. The race-relations minister, George Young, spoke of the need to 'back the good guys, the sensible, moderate, responsible leaders of ethnic groups': otherwise, he said, 'people will turn to the militants'.[20]

In 1981 Herman Ouseley, the Greater London Council's (GLC) first Principal Race Relations Advisor, began what would become a life-long career in official anti-racism. His early accomplishments were, amongst other things, arranging funding for black and anti-racist organisations, establishing race awareness training for council staff and urging other authorities to follow the GLC example.[21] In the same year, Ken Livingstone emerged as the victor in a GLC Labour leadership skirmish. Under Livingstone, the fight against racism included the renaming of streets and public buildings, and the attempt to ban 'racist' Rupert Bear books in schools and the Robertson golliwog motif from jam-jars in council canteens.[22]

Eighties-style municipal anti-racism was at best superficial, and at worst absurd. It turned its back on the real world of politics, policing, deportations and racist attacks, and focused instead on appointing 'race advisors' whose advice amounted to the censorship of words and images, in order that white racism could be 'unlearnt'. The individual became increasingly depicted as the site of racial prejudice, with radical local government assuming the role of moral educator. One ubiquitous GLC poster asked, 'Are you a racist? You'd be much nicer if you weren't'.

In 1986, local authorities ordered employees not to use certain phrases that included the word 'black', and prepared lists of alternatives for 'black spot', 'black market' and 'black list'. As the Workers Against Racism activist Keith Tompson points out in his 1988 book *Under Siege*, the pursuit of such policies in a period of untrammelled racist tension and violence 'created a climate in which more white workers than ever [were] hostile both to black people and to the antiracist cause'.[23]

By the time I was campaigning with ELWAR activists to defend the Stepney Four, things were already changing at a rapid pace. In 1990, our meetings were as likely to discuss the problem of official anti-racism as they were to work out what to do about the latest racist attack or deportation. We were, by now, discussing altogether new problems. Widespread support among young Asians for the campaign against Salman Rushdie's *The Satanic Verses* provided us with a graphic example of anti-racism's absorption into the politics of multiculturalism. Where anti-racism once demanded an end to discrimination, its new municipal and state-funded forms now seemed fixated on cultural sensitivity and vacillated over opposition to the anti-Rushdie protests. Meanwhile, the anti-Rushdie campaign became an opportunity for young Asians to vent their frustration at being left exposed to racism in their daily lives and encounters with the authorities.

In many ways the Rushdie affair initiated, not only new radical identities shaped around Islam, but also the orientation of those on the political left around the celebration of difference. As copies of *The Satanic Verses* formed bonfires, the radical left did not seem to know what to say.

Against the backdrop of this political change and confusion, the Stepney Four were indicative of a new generation of Asians far more at ease with themselves, and prepared to defend their communities. 'Today's Asians walk with a swagger and a strut that was never there a decade ago', noted Kenan Malik in 1995. '[They] wear Chipie jeans and Reeboks, listen to Freakpower and Snoop Doggy Dog, support Arsenal or Blackburn Rovers and on Saturday nights will probably be clubbing at the Astoria or the Wag.'[24] The brash confidence of this new culturally integrated generation, including its determination to fight racists, seemed to become a spur for further police harassment, as young Asian and black men became the new conspicuous upstarts on the block.

Malik discussed his visit to Sara Bibi, eight years on from the time she was beaten with a piece of wood embedded with nails. Her son Mac is doing well and owns a car: 'Mac himself has been stopped, searched and humiliated by police so often that he now drives a BMW with the number plate UPR1X', reported Malik.[25]

Therapeutic politics

Entrenched by decades of hostile confrontation with black and Asian communities, racist attitudes in the police maintained a dogged presence throughout the 1990s. As the century played out, the 1993 murder of Stephen Lawrence and the ensuing campaign for justice gained an increasing political and social prominence.

The New Labour government of 1997 promoted a therapeutic form of governance, formulated through its desire to tackle 'social exclusion' and tackle the underlying 'causes of crime' that, it argued, the previous government had failed to address. The Lawrence campaign presented an opportunity to reconceptualise race relations as a problem of 'community cohesion', with the government addressing the demands of this campaign in a very public way, as part of a self-conscious desire to build trust. Thus the Macpherson Inquiry, launched in 1998, would — in the words of the then Home Secretary Jack Straw — 'allow the concerns of the Lawrence family and others to be fully addressed'.[26]

The sociologist Christopher Kyriakides argues that the Blair government agreed to the Inquiry to stave off the threat the Lawrence campaign posed to the legitimacy of British institutions.[27] Time-honoured fears that brooding resentments would lead to race riots and other forms of social disorder merged with the 'Third Way' thinking of the New Labour government, in an approach termed by Kyriakides 'emotional governance'. The writer James Heartfield explains that '"Third Way" politics is *therapolitics*, appealing to emotion as a means of restraining its effect on dangerous wilful action'.[28] This seems an apt description of the Macpherson Inquiry which, in effect, transformed anti-racism into a therapeutic intervention that sought to suppress untamed, socially-dangerous emotions on both sides.

The Macpherson Inquiry launched a theory of 'institutional racism' which, in explaining the failures of the murder investigation, acknowledged the Lawrence campaign's central grievance. By emphasising 'unwitting' racism, the police could be seen as suffering the same human flaws as the rest of white society. The Inquiry also launched a distinctly therapeutic definition of a racist incident, by emphasising the importance of a victim's or onlooker's perception of an incident in determining whether it should be treated as 'racist'.

The 1999 Macpherson Report heralded a fascinating pendulum swing from the official complicity with, and indifference to, racism that was commonplace in 1970s and 80s, to a veritable enthusiasm for describing society as suffering from the disease of 'racism'. In his endorsement of Macpherson's redefinition of 'institutional racism', Home Secretary Jack Straw announced: '[t]his report does not place a responsibility on someone else; it places a responsibility on each of us.'[29] With racism re-imagined as every individual's 'unwitting prejudice, ignorance, thoughtlessness and racist stereotyping',[30] acts of contrition and redemption became part and parcel of the new 'race relations' orthodoxy.

And as anti-racist campaigners celebrated the Macpherson Report as a hard-won victory, few seemed to notice that the world had already changed. The 'Mac Miah' generation had arrived, as had its African Caribbean equivalent — and an acceptance of diversity was already becoming the norm. In the next period, it would be initiatives led and supported by official *anti*-racism that would play the main role in promoting division and resentment.

Believers versus Deniers

We shoot forwards now to March 2011. The weather is cold, wet and miserable; as I walk south down Cleveland Street the top of London's BT Tower is barely visible. The Tower is my destination and the venue for an intriguing event — an invitation-only 'race debate' held by the Runnymede Trust. The debate had been inspired by a set of articles by black and Asian writers published in *Prospect* magazine under the banner 'Rethinking Race'.[31] In different ways, each writer had demonstrated the negative impact of anti-racist policies; with one, Munira Mirza, going so far as to assert that being black or Asian is 'no longer the significant disadvantage it is often portrayed to be'.[32] '*Prospect* magazine argued in late 2010 that we need to move on from talking about racism', proclaimed the Runnymede Trust's flyer for its debate. 'Are they right?'

The very fact that the Runnymede Trust was prepared to entertain this question was unusual—and indeed, even holding such a debate infuriated some prominent anti-racist campaigners, including former GLC race adviser Lee Jasper. 'I believe that the Runnymede Trust has made a dangerous and unnecessary concession to the racist right in hosting this debate in this way', raged Jasper. '[W]hy on earth are they allowing this right wing white journal [*Prospect*] to set the agenda on race?'[33]

In his own way, Jasper echoed the defining quality of the anti-racism which had come to dominate the period after the 1999 Macpherson Report—encapsulated by the term 'zero tolerance'. The call for 'a zero tolerance approach' increasingly referred, not just to expressions of racism (overt and perceived), but also to 'racism denial'. As we will later explore, Macpherson succeeded in placing the existence of a 'corrosive disease' of racism beyond rebuttal. For many anti-racists, this meant *beyond all doubt*. According to this view, if evidence of racism appears tenuous it doesn't matter because evidence is only the tip of the iceberg; thus, to argue otherwise is to 'deny' the true enormity of the problem.

In 2007, *Guardian* writer Martin Jacques summed up one version of this viewpoint. '[I]f the truth be told, we are a society that is dripping in racism', he argued. 'This is not in the least surprising. For the best part of two centuries, we British ruled the waves, controlled two-fifths of the planet, and believed it was our responsibility to bring civilisation to those who allegedly lacked it... But these attitudes live on in new forms, constantly reproduced in each and every white citizen of this country.'[34] If we believe that the dead hand of history reproduces an ever-present white racism, then even to hint that things have improved becomes 'racism denial'. Of this Lee Jasper had no doubt: 'There is an established culture of routine denial about the reality of social and institutional racism',[35] and Runnymede's decision to hold the debate was thus dangerous because it gave a platform to deniers.

Back in the basement of BT Tower, I am expecting a storm to brew rivalling the one outside. The *Guardian*'s Joseph Harker was to oppose the motion 'Race is no longer a significant disadvantage', and the educationalist Tony Sewell was to speak in support of the motion. Sewell's key point was that the negative experience that black Caribbean boys had at school derived far less from the racist stereotypes and low expectations of white teachers than from the low expectations and self-image they had of themselves. Their experience derived from a cloying 'victim mentality', constantly generating an internalised acceptance of the *idea* that to be black is to be condemned to a life of reduced opportunities.

Sewell offered the audience a brief summary of his project *Generating Genius*,[36] a summer programme for black Caribbean boys with the objective of equipping them with resilience, ambition and a new way of navigating their schooling. Placed on an intensive course dedicated to science, technology, engineering and medicine, the boys began to achieve and then to excel. Back at school, 90 percent of these boys went on to achieve better academic results than their peers. In its narrow way, this project both demolishes the racist idea that something innate about black students leads them to fail, and also challenges the anti-racist idea that institutional racism (specifically the racist assumptions of teachers) leads them to fail. Indeed Sewell could easily have made much of the wider fact that Chinese and Indian pupils do better than white pupils at school, and that black African-descent children do pretty well too.

Sewell's contribution to the Runnymede Trust debate was to suggest that in a fresh 'high expectations' setting, black Caribbean boys can flourish. They stop viewing 'race' as a life-limiting factor and start to challenge the belief that white racist society will forever hold them back. For Sewell's opponents, however, the fresh setting *Generating Genius*[37] provided was simply one that allowed the boys to escape a racism that specifically targeted them.

The fact that five boys from Sewell's project succeeded in gaining places at Oxford University was applauded by the audience as well as his debating opponents. But the biggest cheer came when Joseph Harker stepped up to the podium and declared Sewell's project as 'proof' that racism is the problem. 'The amount of effort it's taken to get those boys to Oxford obviously proves that race must be a significant disadvantage!' exclaimed Harker; for 'if race isn't a disadvantage then why have a programme like Tony's?'[38]

Speaking from the floor, Munira Mirza attempted to sum up a common theme from the *Prospect Magazine* articles that she had guest-edited. 'There are many different ways of looking at social inequality. You can look at race, at gender, at class…', she said. 'But if you look at the statistics, race is one of the least important. If you look at being non-white in this country it is *not* the same thing as being disadvantaged.' This fact is important, Mirza explained, 'because we still have policies [and] pro-grammes that are targeting non-white people and saying that *they* are the ones who are disadvantaged. We still treat non-white people differently, we still have an assumption… that they are victimised'. Such a focus, argued Mirza, 'misunder-stands the importance of class — the fact that black and minority ethnic people are overwhelmingly represented in working-class areas… and it means the solutions we have don't really get to the problems… to fixing the inequalities that do exist'.[39]

Mirza's point about the racialised assumptions driving policy is an important one. In all areas of public life, 'race relations' policies intervene in an attempt to categorise, monitor and fix problems only made visible through the lens of race. However, if we were to remove this race-tinted lens and ask, for example, 'Why do boys of any ethnicity do badly at school?', we would see poverty emerge as a highly significant factor impacting on the school success of black and white children alike.

The caveat Sewell so usefully adds to Mirza's account is that the *idea* of race lingers on as a victim identity long after racism has receded. This victim version of black identity gains its worldview, he argues, from those who reduce low aspiration, low attainment and exclusion to a single explanation — 'racism'. In an age where *anti*-racism now dominates our racial thinking, 'race' can become experienced as a barrier *all by itself*, even in the absence of experiences of actual racism.[40] Where *Generating Genius* seeks to remove this barrier, a great deal of policy acts to bolster it.

Yet in the BT Tower debate, the idea that diminishing levels of racism could be having less and less of a consequence (in terms of victims of racism), while exaggerating levels of racism could be having *a profound effect* (in terms of the promotion of an identity of victimhood) was, it seemed, too preposterous to gain serious consideration. This would, after all, require anti-racist campaigners to consider whether their efforts might be making things worse. The only concession made in this debate was that yes, perhaps, racism had decreased a little. As one audience member put it (paraphrasing Malcolm X), 'if you're being stabbed in the back and they take the knife out one inch would that be progress?' It was an eerily cheerful pessimism that greeted this statement with smiles and applause — as if such a bleak disavowal of decades of progress had made the cause of anti-racism feel as vital as it had in 1981.

A note on 'stereotyping'

For human beings to 'stereotype' other human beings is unavoidable. But the accusation of 'racial stereotyping' is problematic, not least because the term has become interchangeable with the far more barbed accusation of *racist* stereotyping. For example, the stop and search practices of urban police forces in 1980s London were reprehensible not because the act of racial profiling revealed officers as racists — although they may have been. Rather, it was because the police's relentless campaign against black and Asian Londoners was manifestly driven by racism.[41]

And while we might want to debate over how far today's police are trailing behind the curve, times have changed immeasurably since the 1980s. Today, for example, Metropolitan Police Officers instructed to sweep high crime-areas with stops and searches[42] zero in on the same individuals and groups time and again. These are very often working-class areas in which youth maintain a disproportionately visible, public presence. As the criminologist Colin Webster puts it, 'having come to the attention of the police, young people are sucked into a spiral of amplified conflict'.[43] Out of this group it is as likely that police stereotype 'young black men in baggy clothes' as they do young white men in baggy clothes (and, increasingly, young mixed-race men in baggy clothes).

In modern British cities, the 'stereotyping' of young men who happen to be non-white is not the same thing as *racist* stereotyping. Parents of African Caribbean teenage boys will often speak of the way that they tend, at around the ages of 11 or 12, to withdraw and adopt a defiant posture toward school and the world at large.[44] In many cases, they will adopt a physical stance, dress and urban patois style of talk which, by the time the hoods go up, is about as good a stereotype as it gets. Every teacher I know recognises my description of that ubiquitous encounter with a teenage, macho and somewhat sullen version of 'blackness'.

If this is a racial stereotype then it's one that the boys I worked with in Lewisham in south London readily embraced. A few years ago I witnessed an African Caribbean teacher lead a discussion with a group of 15-year-old boys on the 'stereo-typing' they endured. The boys had plenty of examples of being treated with suspicion but they freely admitted that they liked to play on the hoodie-look. As the discussion drew to a close, one boy felt under pressure: 'but you want us to say it's racism, miss!' There was laughter. The last example they had given had involved most in the group. On the way to school an elderly woman, walking towards them, had noticeably clutched her handbag and crossed the road to avoid passing the group. When, after the class, I asked why they had been laughing a boy sheepishly told me that the elderly woman was 'my Jamaican auntie'.

In the anti-racism narrative, 'stereotyping' is a tightly con-trolled buzzword — it must never stray from its assigned script, which holds that white society caricatures black people into a set of negative (and therefore racist) social types. But reality is much more messy than this. The Lewisham boys were, as their teacher would say, 'good boys' — they just liked to pose as bad boys sometimes. They will no doubt look back and remember the fun they had playing up the link between their gangsta-rap image and the reaction it generated. Whether it was a Jamaican auntie imagining them as bag snatchers or a teacher imagining them as the innocent victims of white racial stereotyping, a certain attitude accompanied by a certain look had an irresistible effect. They were able to be, at once, urban folk-devils *and* race-victims.

Given their predilection to focus on the iniquities of stereotyping, it is ironic that the racial stereotypes invoked by ethnic monitoring forms and the endless evocations of black or Black and Minority Ethnic (BME) identity are regarded, by anti-racists, as essential.

Endnotes:

[1]   Ford, R. (2008) 'Is Racial Prejudice Declining in Britain?', *The British Journal of Sociology*, 59(4), p609–36. Accessed 05 June 2014. Available at: http://www.academia.edu/209861/Is_racial_prejudice_ declining_in_Britain. NB: Ford's analysis focuses on two BSA questions asked between 1983 and 1996 dealing with how comfortable white respondents feel about social contact with ethnic minorities. These 'social distance' measures capture attitude change far better than 'self reported' measures (as in the May 2014 NatCen/BSA data release) — they take some account of how we might act on the prejudice we think we hold. Today we are more likely to expand the definition of racial prejudice and view ourselves as bearers of some degree of such prejudice. However, our actions are likely to be increasingly non-discriminatory and anti-racist. Moreover, those few who act on their prejudice now do so without the sanction or tacit approval from the state that they would have once enjoyed.

[2]   Thomas, C. (2010) 'Are Juries Fair?', *Ministry of Justice*. Accessed 05 June 2014. Available at: http://www.justice.gov.uk/downloads/ publications/research-and-analysis/moj-research/are-juries-fair-research.pdf

[3]   See: Ford, R., Jolley, R., Katwala, S., and Mehta, B. (2011) 'The Melting Pot Generation', *British Future*. Accessed 19 May 2014. Available at: http://www.britishfuture.org/wp-content/uploads/ 2012/12/The-melting-pot-generation.pdf. NB: The most recent batch of analysed 2011 Census data not only revealed a country gradually

becoming less white but also that Britain's 'mixed-race' population was now rising at an exponential rate. The snowball effect had almost doubled the 2001 figure of just over 675,000 to over 1.2 million. However, although a million had ticked the box for 'mixed', another million indicated they had 'ethnically mixed parentage' but still chose to tick categories such as 'black' or 'white'. In other words the true figure for 'mixed' was more likely to be in excess of 2 million. The fact that more than half of this figure are under sixteen suggests that our old notions of race may be about to collapse; 'exponential' won't even be able to describe it—tidal-wave may be better. See: Katwala, S. (*Ibid.*, p2); Ford, R. 'The Rise of the Melting Pot Generation' (*Ibid.*, pp4–6); and Eastern, M. (2011) 'Britain: More Mixed Than We Thought', *BBC News*, 06 October. Accessed 18 June 2014. Available at: http://www.bbc.co.uk/news/uk-15164970

4   *Ibid.*

5   See the Runnymede Trust's impressive 'Generation 3.0' video project: 'Birmingham Speaks Out—Isha, aged 14', (2012). Accessed 13 May 2014. Available at: http://www.generation3-0.org/testimonials.html

6   See: Equality and Human Rights Commission (2009) Speech by Trevor Phillips, 'Race in Britain: Ten Years Since the Stephen Lawrence Inquiry', 19 January. Accessed 19 May 2014. Available at: http://www.equalityhumanrights.com/key-projects/race-in-britain/event-ten-years-on-from-the-macpherson-inquiry/stephen-lawrence-speech-institutions-must-catch-up-with-public-on-race-issues/

7   Workers Against Racism (1985) *The Roots of Racism,* London: Junius, p13.

8   See: *Huffington Post UK* (2014) 'Ukip's New Anti-EU Posters Decried As "Racist" And "Inaccurate"', 21 April. Accessed 19 May 2014. Available at: http://www.huffingtonpost.co.uk/2014/04/21/ukip-posters_n_5185245.html

9   A useful analysis of the political undercurrents that gave rise to this shift is made by Kyriakides, C., and Torres, R. (2012) *Race Defaced: Paradigms of Pessimism, Politics of Possibility,* Stanford, California: Stanford University Press.

10   Communities and Local Government: 'Cohesion Research: Statistical Release Number 16, Citizenship Survey 2010/11', p21.

11   *Ibid.*; p22. NB: The Citizenship Survey for 2010/11 was the last before it became victim to government cut-backs.

12   See the Runnymede Race Debate (2013) 'Do Racists Have a Right to be Heard?', RSA Events, 30 January. Accessed 05 June 2014. Available at: http://www.thersa.org/events/audio-and-past-events/2013/the-runnymede-race-debate-do-racists-have-a-right-to-be-heard

13   Malik, K. (1995) 'What Really Angers Young Asians', *The Independent*, 25 June. Accessed 19 May 2014. Available at: http:// www.independent.co.uk/life-style/what-really-angers-young-asians-1588261.html

14   Quoted in: Lewis, N. (1990) 'Defend the Stepney Four!', *WAR News*, Summer issue, p3–4.

15   Malik, K. (2009) *From Fatwa to Jihad: The Rushdie Affair and its Legacy*, London: Atlantic Books, p39.

16   See: *Untold History – 1981* timeline (Channel 4). Accessed 05 June 2014. Available at: http://archive.today/ybiAm

17   Malik, K. (2009) *From Fatwa to Jihad: The Rushdie Affair and its Legacy*, London: Atlantic Books, p39.

18   Lord Scarman (1981) *The Scarman Report: The Brixton Disorders 10–12 April 1981*, London: Pelican.

19   See: http://www.educationengland.org.uk/documents/rampton/rampton1981.html

20   Tompson, K. (1988) *Under Siege: Racial Violence in Britain Today*, London: Penguin Books, p91.

21   *Ibid.*, p98.

22   *Ibid.*, p114.

23   *Ibid.*

24   Malik, K. (1995) 'What Really Angers Young Asians'. *The Independent*, 25 June. Accessed 19 May 2014. Available at: http:// www.independent.co.uk/life-style/what-really-angers-young-asians-1588261.html

25   *Ibid.*

26   See: *BBC Politics 97* (1997) 'Straw Announces Inquiry into Lawrence Murder'. Accessed 21 May 2014. Available at: http://www.bbc.co.uk/news/special/politics97/news/07/0731/lawrence.shtml

27   Kyriakides, C. (2008) 'Third Way Anti-Racism: A Contextual Constructionist Approach', *Ethnic and Racial Studies*, 31(3), pp592–610.

28   Heartfield, J. (2002) *The 'Death of the Subject' Explained*, Sheffield: Hallam Press.

29   See: House of Commons Hansard Debates for 24 February 1999. Accessed 21 May 2014. Available at: http://www.publications.parliament.uk/pa/cm199899/cmhansrd/vo990224/debtext/90224-21.htm

30   Macpherson, W. (1999) *The Stephen Lawrence Inquiry*, UK Government Command Paper 4262–1, Ch 6 s 6.34. Accessed 21 May 2014. Available at: https://www.gov.uk/government/publications/the-stephen-lawrence-inquiry

31   Mirza, M., Sewell, T., Singh, S., Dyer, S., Phillips, M., and Johns, L. (2010) 'Rethinking Race', *Prospect Magazine*, Issue 175, October.

32   *Ibid.*

33   Jasper, L. (2011) 'Runnymede, Race and the Right', Lee Jasper

Official Blog, 16 March. Accessed 18 May 2014. Available at: http://leejasper.blogspot.co.uk/2011/03/runnymede-race-and-right.html

[34] Jacques, M. (2007) 'British Society is Dripping in Racism, but No-one is Prepared to Admit it', *The Guardian*, 20 January. Accessed 17 May 2014. Available at: http://www.theguardian.com/commentisfree/2007/jan/20/comment.0bigbrother

[35] Jasper, L. (2011) 'Runnymede, Race and the Right', Lee Jasper Official Blog, 16 March. Accessed 18 May 2014. Available at: http://leejasper.blogspot.co.uk/2011/03/runnymede-race-and-right.html

[36] See: Runnymede Race Debate 2010, on the motion 'Race is No Longer a Significant Disadvantage in the UK', Accessed 10 June 2014. Available at: http://www.runnymedetrust.org/events-conferences/race-debate.html

[37] For more on the Generating Genius project see: Sewell, T. (2009) *Generating Genius: Black Boys in Love, Ritual and Schooling,* Stoke-on-Trent: Trentham Books. Also see Sewell's debate with Lee Jasper: *Guardian* (2003) 'Look Beyond the Street', 19 July. Accessed 13 June 2014. Available at: http://www.theguardian.com/world/2003/jul/19/race.raceineducation

[38] Runnymede Race Debate 2010, *Op. cit.*

[39] *Ibid.*

[40] In different ways, US writers — brothers Shelby and Claude Steele — have explored how the idea of 'race' can act on individuals in debilitating ways. For their discussion and research on 'race holding' and 'stereotype threat' see: Steele, S. (1998) *A Dream Deferred: The Second Betrayal of Black Freedom in America,* New York: Harper Collins; and Steele, C., and Aronson, J. (1995) 'Stereotype Threat and the Intellectual Test Performance of African Americans', *Journal of Personality and Social Psychology,* 69 (5), pp797–811.

[41] It was not just London: during the 1981 riots in Manchester's Moss Side community workers reported that the police were 'uniformed hooligans beating their truncheons against their vehicles, and chanting slogans such as "Nigger, nigger, nigger — oi, oi, oi!"'. See: Kettle, M., and Hodges, L. (1982) *Uprising: The Police, the People and the Riots in Britain's Cities,* London: Pan Books, p164.

[42] On 'Stop and Search': the ubiquitous line, 'if you are a black person, you are at least six times as likely to be stopped and searched as a white person' (depending on which police power is being cited the figure can rise to '31 times as likely') is misleading. The 'six times' sound bite sidesteps the fact that in London, where only 59.7% of its population are white, black Londoners (who account for half of the total UK black population) make up 13.3% of the population and are, therefore, in London, 3.2 *times as likely to be stopped*. Add to this the fact that black working-class youth (along with white working-class youth) are far more present on the streets and thus 'available'

for police stops and the figures are, arguably, rather less indicative of police 'racist stereotyping'.

[43] See: Webster, C. (2012) 'Different Forms of Discrimination in the Criminal Justice System', in *Criminal Justice v Racial Justice*, London: Runnymede Trust. Accessed 19 May 2014. Available at: http://www.runnymedetrust.org/uploads/publications/pdfs/Criminal JusticeVRacialJustice-2012.pdf

[44] For evidence of black African Caribbean children's sudden drop in attainment levels see: Gillborn, D. (2008) *Racism and Education: Conspiracy or Coincidence?*, London: Routledge, p99. The research, conducted in 2000, suggests that at the age of 5 these children are performing significantly higher than the national average, but that this falls by the age of 11.

Chapter Two

The Ministry of Anti-Racism

For many the 1998 Macpherson Inquiry, despite its failure to bring much clarity over the murder of Stephen Lawrence, was a necessary—even satisfying—excoriation of the police. It was hard, especially for those with the 1980s in mind, not to view Macpherson's condemnation as pay-back; as I indicate in the previous chapter, it is clear that the police had, at the time of Stephen's murder in 1993, a recent history of racism. From then on, as the story unravelled, the part played by police incompetence—with more than a few hints of corruption, complicity and outright racism—merged very easily with what we already knew; and in pronouncing the police as 'institutionally racist', the 1999 Macpherson Report simply *felt* right.

Unfortunately, what many missed at the time was that the report's use of the term 'institutional racism' meant something wholly different to its origins,[1] and that its consequences would extend way beyond a reminder to the police force that black and Asian people deserved equal treatment under the law.

Brian Cathcart, a former deputy editor of the *Independent on Sunday* who had attended the Macpherson Inquiry throughout, endorsed the Report enthusiastically, but was compelled to point out '…as the inquiry moved towards its close it was still the case that no evidence had been produced of a single act of deliberate, malicious racism by a single officer. Nor had it been shown that racism in any form had been the primary cause or one of several primary causes of the failure of the Stephen

Lawrence investigation'.[2] Sir William Macpherson himself made no attempt to assert, least of all prove, that policing policy was racist. 'It is vital to stress', he said, 'that neither academic debate nor the evidence presented to us leads us to say or to conclude that an accusation that institutional racism exists in the Metropolitan Police Service (MPS) implies that the policies of the MPS are racist. No such evidence is before us. Indeed the contrary is true.'[3]

We may feel strongly that police racism played a part in the investigation of Stephen Lawrence's murder. We may feel that the indictment served on the police by the Inquiry was, in any case, justified by years of racist prejudices and practices. Yet the Macpherson Inquiry was not a victory for anti-racism; indeed, it was the launch-pad for a new kind of official orthodoxy, which is every bit as divisive as traditional racism. That is the argument made by this chapter.

Chapter 1 touched on the 'municipal' anti-racism that emerged, first in the Greater London Council (GLC), as a new 'race relations' response to the conflict drenched 1980s. It was evident, even at a time when racism was at its fiercest, that the new official opponents of racism were intent on co-opting black and Asian activists and community leaders into a network of funding-reliant organisations. As Keith Tompson notes, 'while London's black population still suffered abuse, injury and death, its most charismatic advocates found themselves filling out applications and quarrelling over which committee to sit on'.[4] In the process of doing so, the outlook of anti-racist activists shifted evermore toward the official race-relations agenda. From the newly emerging forms of multicultural education to speech codes and bans on jam made by Robertsons, the project of re-educating untutored minds began to unfold.

With the election of the New Labour government in 1997, the official anti-racism that had been largely the preserve of Labour-controlled local authorities now accorded with the 'Third Way' politics of the new government. The management of 'race relations' became increasingly conceived in terms of managing untamed (including 'unwitting') emotions.

Christopher Kyriakides is one of several academics to note how these ideas intertwined and flowed into the 1998 Macpherson Inquiry.[5] Macpherson and his panel of advisers synthesised all that they read and heard from a veritable flotilla of academics, experts and former activists into a set of recommendations that won immediate and unprecedented society-wide approval. Rubber-stamped by Macpherson's 1999 report, the flotilla now had a powerful wind behind it. A year after the report was published, Cabinet Office minister Lord Falconer would comment that Macpherson 'had *proved* that our society and particularly the police are riddled with racism' (my emphasis).[6] Yet as we shall see in this chapter, Macpherson had *proved* nothing of the sort.

For Kyriakides and Torres, the significance of Macpherson was its modernisation of race relations intervention, which successfully redefined racism while reinforcing state authority: 'Macpherson laid the groundwork for the institutionalization of emotional governance.'[7] To understand this process, it is useful to recall key elements of the run-up to the 1998 Inquiry.

The state predicts a riot

The manner in which the murder of Stephen Lawrence escalated into a national *cause célèbre* is worth noting. The day after Stephen's murder his parents were handed anonymous notes listing five names as those of the killers. They passed these on, but the police failed to secure vital evidence from the suspects.[8] On the same day, hearing of the murder, Herman Ouseley of the Commission for Racial Equality (CRE) telephoned the MPS commissioner advising him that the murder should be regarded as a racist crime.[9] Ouseley was later to reflect on the racism of 1993. 'Living in fear', he said, was 'an apt description for the climate of race relations'; while Eltham, Stephen's neighbourhood, was 'one of the "no-go" areas in London for black people'.[10]

Within 20 days of the murder, local Conservative MP Peter Bottomley had also raised 'the worries and concerns of the family and the community' with the MPS commissioner, and the Lawrences had met with Nelson Mandela, who was visiting London. 'The Lawrence tragedy is our tragedy', Mandela told the press, stating that such brutality was commonplace in South Africa, 'where black lives are cheap'.[11]

The excruciating torment that Doreen and Neville Lawrence must have felt across these early days and weeks became intertwined with the rapidly-growing momentum of a high-profile campaign for justice. It was a campaign in which a narrative of brutal social racism and of shocking police failure dovetailed. From the first day, the Lawrence's home had been visited by anti-racist groups including the Anti-Nazi League and the Black Panthers. According to Macpherson Inquiry transcripts, the Anti Racist Alliance (ARA) 'set up camp' at the Lawrence home and 'began to control their communications with outside parties'.[12] The ARA introduced the Lawrences to a young, newly qualified solicitor called Imran Khan. Although all except Khan were eventually asked to leave, Doreen Lawrence was later to pay tribute to the anti-racist groups for making her aware that she was the victim of racism: '…you need groups like the ARA to point out issues to you.'[13]

South-east London at that time had become a focus for anti-racist groups and campaigners.[14] Events had included the murder, in 1991, of 15-year-old Rolan Adams in Thamesmead; the murder, in 1992, of 16-year-old Rohit Duggal in Eltham; and the establishment of the British National Party's (BNP) headquarters and bookshop in Bexley. It was widely believed that there was a connection between the arrival of the BNP in the area and the killings.[15] One shrewd campaigner successfully invited New York's charismatic Reverend Al Sharpton to lead a protest march from the site of Adams's stabbing to the BNP premises just a few miles away.

The Sharpton visit propelled the combination of racist murder, the BNP and south-east London into the headlines — not least because the Conservative Home Secretary Michael Howard had attempted to ban Sharpton's entry into Britain. The march was peaceful but national media coverage escalated an image of dangerous neighbourhoods gripped by racist attitudes and violence. A detailed study by the sociologist Roger Hewitt reveals that the media portrayal was 'deeply resented' by local communities. Much of the news coverage, says Hewitt, painted a picture of a 'uniformly white racist area where hopeless, semi-employed parents reared their hopeless semi-literate children on a diet of racism and brutality'.[16]

In *White Backlash and the Politics of Multiculturalism*, Hewitt describes how the mother of a boy convicted for murdering Rohit Duggal initiated an anti-knife campaign. Her view, as Hewitt puts it, was that 'the problem of teenage conflict was turned into tragedy by the carrying of knives'. The campaign achieved immediate support from the local community but not from anti-racist groups, many of which, according to Hewitt, viewed it 'as a defensive distraction from the central issue of racism'.[17] Hewitt also notes that 'the Duggal family complained of the insensitivity of the ARA and of seeking to control all interviews with the media'.

In this context, it is worth noting a comment that Doreen Lawrence made at the Macpherson Inquiry: 'I personally have never had any racism directed at me… [W]e got on with people. Our immediate next-door neighbour were a white family and we got on with them very well. The children were the same age as my children. We lived in each other's houses and we had no problems.'[18] Had it not been for the part played by the ARA, Imran Khan, Herman Ousley and Nelson Mandela in shaping the racial focus of the Lawrence campaign, this campaign too might have remained exclusively focused on justice for Stephen, and local issues such as street violence.[19]

In the years between Stephen's murder in 1993 and the Macpherson Inquiry in 1998, the Lawrence family campaign gained ever greater prominence via an aborted trial, a fresh police investigation, a failed private prosecution and an inquest. At each stage, the campaign's status as a noble struggle for justice heightened. At the inquest, Doreen Lawrence delivered a statement accusing the judicial system of 'saying to the black community that their lives are worth nothing and the justice system will support anyone, any white person who wishes to commit any crime or even murder, against a black person, you will be protected, you will be supported by the British system'.[20]

But the decisive moment in the campaign came immediately after the inquest when, in February 1997, the *Daily Mail* inaugurated its *Justice for Stephen Lawrence* campaign. On 14 February, the *Mail*'s front page pictured all five suspects with the headline 'Murderers'—'The *Mail* accuses these men of killing. If we are wrong, let them sue us'. The next day the newspaper released 'a chilling series of images' obtained from a secret police surveillance camera which revealed 'the bloodlust of the Lawrence case gang'.[21]

Speaking in 2012, former Home Secretary Jack Straw recalled how the Lawrence family and their 'very impressive' advisors influenced his decision to order the Macpherson Inquiry in 1998. Another key influence had been the *Mail*'s front page, published just four months before he became home secretary. 'I saw the Lawrence inquiry as a means not only of changing the attitudes and character of the police, but of British society', Straw told the Radio Four programme *The Long View*.[22]

The Lawrence campaign and its mounting sense of grievance had gained the unflinching attention of Britain's political elite. The campaign contained all the elements needed to stir latent fears of 'racial disorder' and focus minds on the need to restore trust amongst 'the black community'. Amidst mounting media and public demands that 'something must be done', the idea took root that swathes of Britain were still trapped inside the racial tensions of 1981. Macpherson would later speak of '[the] existence of a sub-culture of obsessive violence, fueled by racist prejudice and hatred against black people'.[23] The apparent racist savagery of the murder suspects and the unwitting racism of the police were all part of the same psycho-social problem to which the state must quickly be seen to attend.

The Macpherson Inquiry was to become Lord Scarman's unfinished business—New Labour style. As Hewitt points out, political intention and public revulsion 'became synchronized in the hearings of the inquiry', which were deliberately made public and conducted in the heart of south London.[24] In his report, Macpherson speaks of society's need 'to purge itself of racial prejudice and violence'. He concludes his second chapter with an extract from Scarman's commentary on the 1981 riots. 'Urgent action is needed', ran the Scarman extract, 'if [racial disadvantage] is not to become an endemic, ineradicable disease threatening the very survival of our society... racial disadvantage and its nasty associate racial discrimination, have not yet been eliminated. They poison minds and attitudes; they are, as long as they remain, and will continue to be a potent factor of unrest.'

'It is a sad reflection upon the intervening years', commented Macpherson, 'that in 1998–99 those extracted words have remained relevant throughout both parts of our Inquiry.'[25]

'We taught Macpherson and Macpherson taught the world':[26] The role of expert anti-racists

William Macpherson, son of a brigadier, once a captain of the Scots Guards, received something of an education over the course of his inquiry into Stephen Lawrence's murder. By its start in March 1998, he had read over 50 written submissions from an assortment of invited experts, academics, race equality councils and community groups. No fewer than 70 individuals appeared before the Inquiry, including a member of the Black Lawyers Association by the name of Peter Herbert.[27] Singled out for their especially 'helpful' contributions (in the form of written submissions or witness testimony) were Sir Herman Ouseley, the '1990 Trust' (Lee Jasper and colleagues), Dr (now Professor) Benjamin Bowling, Professor Simon Holdaway and Dr Robin Oakley. All put forward explanations for the abject failure of the police in the Lawrence and other cases that used the term 'institutional racism'.[28]

It was Dr Oakley's explanation that appeared to make the biggest impression. The 1981 Scarman Report, argued Oakley, had failed to draw out the significance of Lord Scarman's own words. Despite dismissing the idea that the police suffered from anything he would call 'institutional racism', Scarman had nonetheless spoken of a racism that was 'hidden and unconscious' and 'unwitting'. Scarman had said, 'Unwitting racism can arise because of lack of understanding, ignorance or mistaken beliefs. It can arise from well intentioned but patronising words or actions. It can arise from unfamiliarity with the behaviour or cultural traditions of people or families from minority ethnic communities. It can arise from racist stereotyping of black people as potential criminals or troublemakers'.[29]

For Oakley, this formulation was the very essence of institutional racism because it grasped the covert, indirect, unintentional dimension that 1990s racism took—thus 'its most important challenging feature' was its 'predominantly hidden character' and its 'inbuilt pervasiveness'. 'It could be said that institutional racism in this sense is in fact pervasive throughout the culture and institutions of the whole of British society, and is in no way specific to the police service', said Oakley.[30] The Macpherson Report is unclear how Dr Oakley knew this to be a 'fact'.[31]

Confession and redemption, racism and 'denial'

In his report, Macpherson indicates that the panel was 'heartened' and 'encouraged' by any police submission which displayed 'an unequivocal acceptance of the problem of institutional racism'.[32] Thus the views of Chief Constable David Wilmot, who 'plainly accepted' police institutional racism, were warmly welcomed. Wilmot accepted that within the Greater Manchester Police 'there was still institutional racism, both in an "internalised" way (just as in society) and an overt way'. The new president of the Association of Chief Police Officers (ACPO), Chief Constable John Newing, stated: 'I define institutional racism as the racism which is *inherent in wider society* which shapes our attitudes and behaviour… In the police force there is a distinct tendency for officers to stereotype people' (my emphasis).[33]

Macpherson concluded that it was institutional racism, rather than incompetence or corruption, that explained 'the lack of urgency' of the murder investigation.[34] It explained why officers refused to see the murder as 'purely' motivated by racism and, nationwide, it explained the disparity in stop and search figures as well as 'the under-reporting of racial incidents'.[35]

We can only guess at what stage Macpherson and his panel became struck by a certain historical gravity to their Inquiry that extended far beyond probing the botched police investigation of the Lawrence murder. It was indeed 'a watershed' moment.[36] This was not only a chance to execute Scarman's unfinished business and articulate the missing conceptual dimension of 'institutional racism'. In doing so it was also a chance to advance a theory of racism that illuminated its presence in the police while avoiding too damning an indictment on an institution reliant on public trust. After all, it was implied, the police merely reflected the 'unwitting' racism of white society at large; they were as humanly flawed as everyone else.

The outlook that seems to have moved the Macpherson panel was that racism was as much a part of the fabric of British society in 1998 as it ever had been. The only difference was that it was less overt—that it had in some way or other (which no one had yet quite articulated) gone underground. In this regard, the ideas of Eighties municipal anti-racism and incumbent academic theories on re-educating and reprogramming untutored minds now seemed to chime perfectly with Macpherson's recommendations.

In contrast to those who announced their unequivocal acceptance of 'institutional racism' (as hidden, unconscious, unwitting and inherent in wider society), Metropolitan police commissioner Sir Paul Condon was denounced for his failure to do so. In the Inquiry, Macpherson's panel insisted, again and again, that Condon declare his unequivocal acceptance. He refused. The fury of the panel and the crowd in the public gallery became feverish. 'You have told us ten times. Please don't tell us again that you are not in denial', exclaimed panel member Dr Richard Stone. He persisted: '…you are nearly there… the door is open. It is like when Winnie Mandela was challenged in the Truth Commission in South Africa... I say to you now, just say "Yes, I acknowledge institutional racism in the police" and then in a way the whole thing is over.'[37]

Condon's steadfast refusal to accept that the murder of Stephen Lawrence was 'purely' or 'solely' motivated by racism was regarded by the Inquiry as itself clear evidence of institutional racism. 'Methinks the Commissioner doth protest too much', was Dr Stone's recollection in 2013. '[T]he public left us in no doubt about their opinion on these comments and needed to be calmed by Sir William.'[38]

Macpherson's final definition of institutional racism is worth quoting in full:

> For the purposes of the inquiry the concept of institutional racism which we apply consists of:
>
> The collective failure of an organisation to provide an appropriate and professional service to people because of their colour, culture, or ethnic origin. It can be seen or detected in processes, attitudes and behaviour which amount to discrimination through unwitting prejudice, ignorance, thoughtlessness and racist stereotyping which disadvantage minority ethnic people. It persists because of the failure of the organisation openly and adequately to recognise and address its existence and causes by policy, example and leadership. Without recognition and action to eliminate such racism it can prevail as part of the ethos or culture of the organisation. It is a corrosive disease.

Some radical commentators, like Jenny Bourne at the Institute of Race Relations (IRR), noted a problem with Macpherson's definition. For Bourne the definition had, rather unhelpfully, reduced racism to individual attitudes and behaviour. 'But all that Macpherson was trying to say', she argued, 'is that if you work in an organisation whose structures, cultures and procedures are racist, it is inevitable that individuals who work there should be contaminated by such racism.'[39]

In fact, Macpherson had explicitly placed the relationship between racism and organisational structures the other way round. For Macpherson it was 'vital to stress' that while 'institutional racism' existed in the police this should not imply 'that the policies of the MPS are racist'.[40] Rather, said Macpherson, 'it is in the implementation of policies and, in the words and actions of officers acting together that racism may become apparent'. Transposed to society as a whole, 'institutional racism' is, according to Macpherson, what happens when an infected mass of people (that's you, me and the masses) go to work for organisations. The leadership and policies of an organisation only become complicit in institutional racism when there is a failure to recognise and address its existence.

The important point for Bourne was that the Macpherson Report must be defended against its enemies — 'philosophical sniffer-dogs' who deride his conception of 'institutional racism' as political correctness and, in ridiculing 'unwitting racism' as unprovable, dismiss the Inquiry as being no better than a Stalinist show-trial.[41] Yet while it is true that the term 'political correctness' can be used glibly to shut down debate, so too can the counter-accusation of a 'right-wing backlash'. In the years since Macpherson, the accusation of 'backlash' — often tied-in with phrases like 'the racist right' — has had a far greater effect on silencing debate. In any case, there were very few examples of criticism of Macpherson from those who had previously been vociferous about multiculturalism and the 'loony left', while academics and serious printed journalism fell silent too.

The criticism-shrivelling force-field that Macpherson had mounted at the Inquiry and inscribed within his self-fulfilling theory of institutional racism offered a clear indication of the fate that awaits dissenters. To this day, anyone in public life who values their career will think twice before criticising the Macpherson Report, and it has escaped a great deal of the serious intellectual challenge it might otherwise have received.[42]

Race crimes: a matter of intention or perception?

The murder of Stephen Lawrence has been subject to countless descriptions since it occurred on the evening of 22 April 1993. However, few seem ever to mention a witness to the murder named Royston Westbrook. As Stephen and his friend Duwayne Brooks arrived at a bus stop on Eltham's Well Hall

Road, Stephen walked towards Dickson Road. It was then that a group of white youths appeared on the opposite side of the road. Duwayne called out to ask Stephen if a bus was coming. It is thought one of the youths heard Duwayne and called out 'What, what! Nigger!' The group rushed across the road and engulfed Stephen; he was stabbed twice but managed to run up the road with Duwayne before collapsing.

Duwayne's 999 call from a phone box opposite the position where Stephen fell was received at 10.43pm and the police arrived seven minutes later. Even before a police car and ambulance arrived, members of the public came to give Stephen what assistance they could. These included an off-duty police constable and his wife who were passing in their car. There had been several witnesses at the bus stop, who boarded the bus at exactly the moment the commotion occurred. The Macpherson Report notes the testimony of Royston Westbrook, a white man in his thirties who was on his way home after finishing his evening shift as a hospital support worker. 'As he got on the bus', says the Report, 'he felt a shiver of apprehension when he thought to himself that the attack seemed so motiveless that it might have been levelled at him if the two boys had not been there.'[43]

By the time Macpherson wrote his report he was, as we have seen, firmly convinced that the actions of the police in the Lawrence case were infected by *institutional racism*. Its *a priori* existence, within the police and wider society, had been confirmed by a raft of expertise and experience. Evidence of its existence was also deduced by Macpherson from the refusal of officers to accept that the murder had been motivated 'purely' by racism. However, at the start of the Inquiry, Macpherson held no such view.

In his opening address, counsel for the inquiry Edmund Lawson QC described the suspects as 'violent thugs' who 'did not limit their gratuitously violent attacks to black victims'.[44] Under cross-examination from Michael Mansfield, barrister for the Lawrence family, Detective Sergeant John Davidson said, 'I believe it was thugs attacking anyone, as they had done on previous occasions with other white lads... They were thugs who were out to kill, not particularly a black person but anybody and I believe that to this day that that was thugs, not racism, just pure bloody-minded thuggery'.[45]

By 1993 the police had been using the Association of Chief Police Officers (ACPO) definition of a racist incident for several years: that is, 'any incident which included an allegation of racial motivation made by any person'. As the above quotations indicate, the question of whether Stephen's murder was racially motivated formed an important element of the discussion during the Macpherson Inquiry, with different perspectives offered as to whether Stephen was targeted because he was black, or simply because he was there. Continually, the Inquiry was confronted with the difficulty of trying to establish what was going on in the killers' minds, which may or may not have been revealed by what they said at the time.

One of the most important outcomes of Macpherson was to shift the definition of a racist incident, to make the *perception* of racial motivation, by the victim or onlooker, much more central. Thus, Recommendation 12 of Macpherson's report states: 'A racist incident is any incident perceived to be racist by the victim or any other person.' Meanwhile, Recommendation 13 and 14 made clear that such incidents included crimes and non-crimes and should be 'universally adopted by the police, local government and other relevant agencies'.

The definition was no longer a guideline to ensure allegations were taken seriously: it was now much more. A racist attack is no longer defined according to what might be going on in the perpetrator's mind, but according to what is going on in other people's minds. And this is a recipe for disaster.

From government offices to school playgrounds, the definition of a racist incident is interpreted as follows: 'if the victim or anyone thinks it's racism, *it is*.' The obvious subjectivity inferred by the definition became an open invitation for 'third-party victimhood'; to take offence on behalf of someone else. As indicated by the debate over Stephen's murder, when dealing with the realm of perception we are likely to solicit a wide range of competing interpretations about whether something is racist or not, which serves mainly to foment confusion and defensiveness. This is the subject of the remaining chapters.

Endnotes:

1   When the American civil rights activist Stokey Carmichael first used the term 'institutionalised racism', he was referring to the oppressive power of state apparatus. But this is not what Macpherson means by 'institutional racism'.

2   Cathcart, B. (1999) *The Case of Stephen Lawrence,* London: Penguin Viking, p357.

3   Macpherson, W. (1999) *The Stephen Lawrence Inquiry,* UK Government Command Paper 4262-1, Ch 6.24.

4   Tompson, K. (1988) *Under Siege: Racial Violence in Britain Today,* London: Penguin, p91.

5   Kyriakides, C. (2008) 'Third Way Anti-Racism: A Contextual Constructionist Approach', *Ethnic and Racial Studies*, 31(3).

6   Cited by Dennis, N. (2000) 'Crime and Punishment: "Lawrence Inquiry Failed Britain"', *Daily Telegraph*, 15 September. Accessed 14 May 2014. Available at: http://www.telegraph.co.uk/news/uknews/1355489/Crime-and-Punishment-Lawrence-inquiry-failed-Britain.html

7   Kyriakides C., and Torres, R. (2012) *Race Defaced: Paradigms of Pessimism, Politics of Possibility,* Stanford, California: Stanford University Press, p154.

8   See: Stone, R. (2013) *Hidden Stories of the Stephen Lawrence Inquiry, Personal Reflections,* Bristol: The Policy Press (Kindle).

9   Dennis, N., Erdos, G., and Al-Shahi, A. (2000) *Racist Murder and Pressure Group Politics: The Macpherson Report and the Police,* London: Civitas, pxii.

10 Ouseley, H. (2012) 'Stephen Lawrence Verdicts Must Establish New Standards for All Hate Crimes', *Guardian*, 3 January. Accessed 14 May 2014. Available at: http://www.theguardian.com/commentisfree/2012/jan/03/stephen-lawrence-new-standards-hate-crime

11 Dennis, N., Erdos, G., and Al-Shahi, A. (2000) *Racist Murder and Pressure Group Politics: The Macpherson Report and the Police,* London: Civitas, pxii.

12 *Ibid.*, p64. Here the authors are citing Lawrence Inquiry appendices 'Mr E. Lawson QC appearing on behalf of the inquiry', p61.

13 *Ibid.*

14 See: Hewitt, R. (2005) *White Backlash and the Politics of Multiculturalism*, Cambridge: Cambridge University Press.

15 *Ibid.*, p45.

16 *Ibid.*, p47.

17   *Ibid.*, p50.

18   Macpherson, W. (1999) *The Stephen Lawrence Inquiry*, 'Statement of Doreen Lawrence, 8 March 1998', UK Government Command Paper 4262–II (Revised), London: The Stationary Office. Cited in Dennis *et. al.* (2000) *Op. cit.*, p1.

19   The 'Acourt Gang' were something of 'a local issue' all by themselves. They were a notorious group of adolescents (aged 16 to 17 years old at the time of Stephen's murder) who were feared and despised on the central Greenwich estates (see: Hewitt, R. (2005) *Op. cit.*, p54: 'its members were well known for a violence which extended beyond racially motivated attacks'). Neil and Jamie Acourt had been linked to the stabbing of a white youth (Lee Pearson) in 1991 and Neil Acourt was allegedly present, along with David Norris, at the stabbing of another white youth (Stacey Benefield) in 1993 (just a few weeks before the Lawrence murder itself). Moreover, this friendship-group's reputation for violent aggression toward randomly selected victims was well known in Eltham. The Acourts in particular were nicknamed 'the Eltham Krays'. Chapters 7, 8 and 9 of the Macpherson Report discuss these matters.

20   Macpherson, W. (1999) *The Stephen Lawrence Inquiry*, UK Government Command Paper 4262–I, London: The Stationary Office, Ch 42.13.

21   See: Wright, S. (2012) 'The *Mail's* Victory: How Stephen Lawrence's killers were finally brought to justice years after our front page sensationally branded the evil pair murderers', *Daily Mail*, 3 January. Accessed 19 May 2014. Available at: http://www.dailymail.co.uk/news/article-2080159/Stephen-Lawrence-case-How-killers-finally-brought-justice.html

22   BBC Radio 4 (2012) *The Long View.* Accessed 19 May 2014. Available at: http://www.bbc.co.uk/programmes/b019f9h7

23   Macpherson, W. (1999) *Op. cit.*, Ch 2.18.

24   Hewitt, R. (2005) *Op. cit.*, p54.

25   Macpherson, W. (1999) *Op. cit.*, Ch 2.20.

26   Sivanandan, A. (2000) 'Macpherson and After', Institute of Race Relations, 19 February. Accessed 07 June 2014. Available at: http://www.irr.org.uk/news/macpherson-and-after/

27   At Part 2 of the inquiry Herbert does no more than to answer a question on the usefulness of the term 'institutional racism': '...[T]he fact that there is racism which is the common experience of the black community must be recognised. Institutional is the academic, and I suppose the logical label if the policies and practices of an organisation provide that context for it to exist.' See: transcripts from the Macpherson Inquiry (Part 2, Day 5, p576) posted by Dr Richard Stone on his blog. Accessed 12 June 2014. Available at: http://richardstonesli.files.wordpress.com/2012/02/d005slp2.pdf

28   These explanations came via either written submissions and, in
     some cases, witness testimony. For the latter see: http://
     richardstonesli.wordpress.com/transcripts/, *ibid.*
29   Macpherson, W. (1999) *Op. cit.*, Ch 6.17.
30   *Ibid.*, Ch 6.31.
31   Cited in Dennis, N., Erdos, G., and Al-Shahi, A. (2000) *Op. cit.*, p109–
     11; see also: Macpherson, W. (1999) *Op. cit.*, Ch 6.31. See also:
     'Institutional Racism and Police Service Delivery' (Dr Oakley's
     submission to the inquiry). Accessed 12 June 2014. Available at:
     file:///C:/Users/Ady/Downloads/Instracism&pol98.pdf
32   Macpherson, W. (1999) *Op. cit.*, Ch 6.49.
33   *Ibid.*, Ch 6.50.
34   *Ibid.*, Ch 6.45.
35   *Ibid.*
36   See: 'Statement by Jack Straw to the Stephen Lawrence Inquiry'
     (1999). Accessed 22 May 2014. Available at: http://www.
     publications.parliament.uk/pa/cm199899/cmhansrd/vo990224/
     debtext/90224-21.htm
37   Quoted by Stone, R. (2013) *Op. cit.*
38   *Ibid.*
39   Bourne, J. (2001) 'The Life and Times of Institutional Racism', *Race &
     Class*, 43 (7), p19.
40   Macpherson, W. (1999) *Op. cit.,* Ch 6.24.
41   Bourne, J. (2001) *Op. cit.,* p18.
42   Dennis, N., Erdos, G., and Al-Shahi, A. (2000) *Op. cit.,* p143.
43   Macpherson, W. (1999) *Op. cit.,* Ch 21.23.
44   Cited in Dennis, N., Erdos, G., and Al-Shahi, A. (2000) *Op. cit.,* p78.
45   Macpherson, W. (1999) *Op. cit.,* Ch 19.34. NB: At the time of writing
     (May 2014), Davidson has been subject to fresh allegations of
     corruption in relation to the Stephen Lawrence investigation. See:
     http://www.theguardian.com/uk-news/2014/mar/06/stephen-
     lawrence-case-suspects-supergrasses. The Macpherson Inquiry had
     clearly been troubled about the possible motives behind DS
     Davidson's investigative deficiencies but, as a more recent Home
     Office independent review by Mark Ellison QC has pointed out, 'the
     Inquiry also found that there were examples of DS Davidson pur-
     suing the prosecution of the murder suspects with some vigour'.
     See: Ellison, M. (2014) *The Stephen Lawrence Independent Review:
     Summary of Findings,* 06 March, London: HMSO, p6. Accessed on 11
     June 2014. Available at: https://www.gov.uk/government/
     uploads/system/uploads/attachment_data/file/287030/stephen_
     lawrence_review_summary.pdf

Chapter Three

Diversity Rules

In the task of clarifying some of the tangled complexity surrounding what we mean by 'race', 'cultural difference' and 'diversity' today, I am indebted to the writer, public intellectual and veteran anti-racist activist Kenan Malik. A prolific interrogator of these and many other themes, Malik has cut a path through the confusion and polarising stalemate evident in so much of the debate on race and multiculturalism. For Malik, the pathway opens up once we separate 'diversity' as lived experience from the frequently divisive attempts to 'manage' diversity at a policy level.

Many of us would agree with Malik that the experience of living in a multicultural, multi-ethnic, *plural* society awash with different customs and outlooks is a welcome one; something innately possessed with the potential to make our world a better place. By contrast, the consequence of attempts to manage this diversity, under the banner of 'multiculturalism' or 'anti-racism', is, as Malik puts it, 'to seal people into ethnic boxes and to police the boundaries'.[1] The British state's management of diversity is, therefore, a very different matter precisely because it is mired in the racialised politics of difference.

For modern-day anti-racists, the goal of transcending race sought by campaigners in the past is condemned as utopian dreaming if not pure anathema. 'Colour-blindness' — the aspiration to see past race — is contemptuously cast as both racism-blindness and an offence to identity. By embracing racial identity as something essential to individual and group self-esteem — as something that must never be disrespected or offended — modern day anti-racists conjure fresh struggles from a world of seemingly endless racial slights. Their colour-coded outlook places the dominant white 'culture' as the serial perpetrator of racial offence — from wounding racist insult to wounding cultural criticism.

In the lexicon of anti-racism the domination of white society over its ethnic minority citizens entails, as exponents of Critical Race Theory (CRT) put it, 'hidden operations of power' deeply ingrained within a culture of white privilege.[2] Amidst this spectre of racial domination, 'racism' need not refer to explicit acts of hatred or discrimination: it simply floats in the ether permanently signalling its presence to the oppressed 'Other'.

In this regard, the politics of identity and difference, and the policies that flow from this, can be understood as the old *racial thinking* by other means. In other words, these are politics that are possessed with the innate potential to divide us along racial lines.

'Diversity is important', explains Malik, 'because it allows us to break out of our culture-bound boxes, to expand our horizons, to compare and contrast different values, beliefs, lifestyles, make judgments upon them and decide which may be better and which may be worse...'.[3] Malik's evocation of 'diversity' — as a messy, exciting flux of social interaction which necessarily involves cultural and ideological clashes — is exactly what advocates of the post-Macpherson, anti-racist outlook fear. Rather, diversity is viewed as a good only when conceived of as a patchwork of fixed 'cultural' differences, in which clashes and conflicts are managed and minimised.

Pondering a cultural market-place brimming with ideological exchange triggers the same ambivalence amongst modern anti-racists as does pondering the way that racial difference has been melted away by inter-ethnic marriage. It reeks of assimilation and, as such, a threat to its core value of respect for 'difference'. The conservative outlook of the new anti-racism is, then, a combination of a pragmatic, top-down managerialism. Both fear the consequences of 'race relations' coming undone: 'unmanaged' diversity can, it is assumed, only incite racism, stir racial offence and trigger racial discord. It shouldn't surprise us, then, that the new anti-racism tends to equate criticism of minority cultural tradition and religion with racism. Nor should it surprise us that managing diversity has become inextricably linked to the regulation of speech and the policing of offence-giving.

As we discuss below and in the following chapters, today's 'diversity' rules guide us in the exact opposite direction to freedom of speech, thought and expression. Post-Macpherson anti-racism has supercharged this trend, generating an ever-greater social pressure to conform to its tenets over correct speech and correct thought and to censure, sanction or morally condemn those who transgress. The anti-racist *goodthinker* is, to adapt Orwell's definition from *Nineteen Eighty-Four*, one who strongly adheres to the contemporary etiquette of racial correctness — or at least appears to do so.[4]

However, a contradiction that occasionally arises is who, from a world so permeated with unwitting racism, can the enlightened guardians of anti-racist thought ever be? It seems the answer to this conundrum is Diversity Rule #1: racism is a social disease, we are all vulnerable to it, and therefore the need for an 'independent' moral arbiter — in the form of policies, guidelines and laws — is cemented. The *enlightened few* will come and go and, sometimes ingloriously, they will have to go with heads bowed (perhaps, back to the classroom, where a diversity trainer awaits). But the regulations stay, and grow.

Managing diversity

In the first chapter we discussed how the official 'municipal' anti-racism emerging in the 1980s, indelibly imbued with the events of 1981, became a major influence on the body of knowledge, experience and expertise presented to the 1998 Macpherson Inquiry. This, in turn, shaped the Inquiry's outlook. Macpherson and his panel became convinced that the fires of the 1980s were still burning in late 1990s Britain, albeit in a largely invisible way. A belief in the absolute truth of Britain's 'corrosive disease' became so fervent that anything seeming to deny it became regarded as further evidence of racism's insidious presence.

However, this was not a cultural trend exclusively motivated by the various strands articulated and synthesised at the Macpherson Inquiry, in its subsequent report and in the amended legislation it inspired. The new anti-racist outlook dovetailed with, arguably, some of the worst cultural trends of our times — namely, an aversion to any speech perceived hateful and/or harmful, and a desire to have this regulated. Identity politics helped to reinstate what should, by now, have been discredited ideas about race. Those earlier, racialised formulations over 'natural' and 'irreconcilable' differences became re-branded by well-intentioned anti-racists as a progressive demand — *the right to be different.*

In the civil rights struggles of the past, the victims of race discrimination demanded their right to be treated, not differently, but *equally* — to be accorded the same rights as everyone else. In place of the discrimination meted out by old-fashioned official racism, modern-day official anti-racism discriminates on the basis that you have to treat people differently to treat them equally; that is, you have to manage diversity by recognising individual and group *racial* (read 'cultural') identity. The result has been to racialise communities, encourage a proliferation of individual and group grievance, and foster intense competition for public recognition and protection.

The interaction between, on one hand, elite fears over racial disorder — triggered by anything from untamed hate to ill-considered words or criticism — and, on the other, growing demands for protection and remedy, ends up merging with a more generally censorious trend in twenty-first-century society. Here, the freedom to express — to speak, write, sing and even think what we like — and to confront the speech we don't like by using the same freedom becomes curtailed. The resolution to clashes of opinion is seen increasingly to lie, not in the public arena, but through official arbitration.

In this vein, Recommendation 39 of the Macpherson Report urges the state to consider a law to allow prosecution of 'offences involving racist language or behaviour' which can be proven to have taken place 'otherwise than in a public place'. The distinctly eerie prospect of family members reporting one another to the authorities emerges into view.[5] The ease with which Macpherson could make such a recommendation without triggering an avalanche of controversy is testament to how far our defence of everyday freedom finds itself on the back foot. This is particularly so when pitted against calls for a robust 'zero tolerance approach' in stamping out racism 'in all its forms'.

On hearing of the case of a school playground argument that ended with the prosecution of a 10-year-old boy on a 'racially aggravated public order' charge, the respected author and *Guardian* writer Cameron Duodi felt moved to say, 'it is the duty of the authorities to stamp it out. And if that means taking a 10- or 11-year-old racist before the courts, so be it'.[6]

In what follows, we will consider how post-Macpherson 'official' anti-racism blossomed into an all-pervasive moral code. Backed by legislation demanding 'good relations between persons of different racial groups', public institutions set about policing the 'unwitting'. And yet, in every example we consider, the consequence of anti-racism is to paralyse social interaction, and foster a sense of estrangement.

The diversity industry

The impact of the Macpherson Inquiry has been far reaching. Alongside changes to the police force and the criminal justice system, Macpherson's findings were quickly incorporated into new legislation. The Race Relations (Amendment) Act 2000 extended existing race legislation to cover, not just the police, but more than 45,000 public bodies, including state schools and universities. The Act imposed a general duty on all these bodies to 'have due regard to the need to eliminate unlawful discrimination and to promote equality of opportunity and good relations between persons of different racial groups'.

A rejuvenated industry of diversity training and ethnic monitoring ensued. Covering workplaces, schools and local authorities, the industry took its cue from a plethora of government advice and guidance that invariably quoted directly from Macpherson. One favoured quotation ran: 'How society rids itself of [racist] attitudes is not something we can prescribe, except to stress the need for education and example at the youngest age, and an overall attitude of "zero tolerance" of racism within our society.'[7] Books on combating the racism of infants began to appear, bolstered by Macpherson's certainty that, as Babette Brown, founder of the Early Years Trainers Anti-Racist Network (EYTARN), put it, '…racism starts among the very young and becomes deeply ingrained'.[8] With reference to the Lawrence murder suspects, Brown asked: 'when they were young children were they given opportunities to unlearn any discriminatory messages they had already learnt?'[9]

Opportunities to 'unlearn' racism and to value diversity proliferated across the public sector but were by no means confined to it. By the 1990s, Diversity Training—especially in the USA—was already fast becoming the must-have ostentatious feature of any modern, forward-looking organisation, from universities to big business. As one sociologist notes, 'when the World Bank organises "Diversity and Tolerance Workshops" it is evident that diversity has become truly sacralised'.[10]

In practice, diversity training has caused many to scoff, and some to be openly critical. Arwa Mahdawi, a columnist for the *Guardian* online, describes the term 'diversity', when applied to the workplace, as 'a divisive and rather weird concept'.[11] Ostensibly, diversity training was first used to improve productivity by enhancing relations between ethnically and culturally diverse workforces or enhancing a workforce's relations with the public. Many would agree that diversity training and special diversity programmes quickly became essential for organisations needing to demonstrate good practice while reducing the risk of race discrimination litigation, rather than because they were shown to contribute positively to employees' experience.

In fact, far from making the workplace more harmonious, diversity or 'equalities' training soon earned a reputation for generating employee resentment. The transparently shallow and manipulative use of therapeutic techniques fuel the sense that diversity training is an intrusive, tokenistic gesture, and many recipients of training note the irony that, once back at work, the experience of having been 'trained' in diversity seems to create a sense of workplace division that had not previously existed. As the workplace becomes more 'trained', the grievances that lead to complaints and employment tribunals proliferate, which in turn spurs employers on to call in diversity consultants who recommend, among other things, more or different types of training.

Arwa Mahdawi cites the leading American diversity trainer Peter Bregman, who now accepts that most of his industry's output has been counter-productive. Writing in *Psychology Today*, Bregman offers two reasons why organisations commission training: 'one is to prevent lawsuits. The other is to create an inclusive environment in which each member of the community is valued, respected and can fully contribute their talents.'[12] For UK public institutions we might add a third—to demonstrate compliance with legislation. Bregman describes how discussions with training participants gradually confirmed 'a feeling that had been pestering me for years: Diversity training doesn't extinguish prejudice. It promotes it'.

Bregman started to notice that sessions on the 'correct' language became the butt of jokes as did sessions that dealt with group categories. 'People aren't prejudiced against real people,' says Bregman, 'they're prejudiced against categories. "Sure, John is gay," they'll say, "but he's not like other gays". Their problem isn't with John, but with gay people in general. Categories are dehumanizing. They simplify the complexity of a human being. So focusing people on the categories increases their prejudice.'

It is tempting to propose that diversity training simply be replaced with more social events—because it's in the informal, private sphere that we instinctively remove the barriers that separate us and discover common bonds. We also need the opportunity to differ, clash, joke and banter with one another and, in doing so, experience a falling away of the need for inter-personal grievance procedures. With our working and social lives increasingly experienced as atomised and bereft of communality, diversity training exploits this vacuum and may even feel good at the time. But ultimately it leaves many feeling their emotions and interpersonal relations are being micro-managed — if not manipulated. And as we consent to handing over the smooth management of our interpersonal workplace relations to external governance, it follows that any grievance we experience will require a formal remedy. As the American academic Elisabeth Lasch-Quinn has noted, diversity training ends up nurturing hypersensitivity. We become, notes Lasch-Quinn, 'sensitive to all the wrong things at all the wrong times'.[13]

Of workplace diversity-boosting schemes, Mahdawi finds the social categories that are left out something of a give-away. 'The definitions of diversity tend to be skin-deep, about differences you can see — and stick on the cover of your cor-porate brochure', says Mahdawi. She adds: 'because diversity credentials are something companies like to show off, it tends to help to focus on the more marketable minorities.' Citing US research, Mahdawi ridicules the selective 'diversity' of positive discrimination schemes, none of which take account of the poor career prospects of those deemed 'unattractive'. 'And God/ Allah, don't even get me started on the fat', snaps Mahdawi. 'Women: when it comes to earning potential it seems you can never be too thin.'[14]

The category so obviously left out of 'diversity' is, as Mahdawi points out, class. Educated in a public school and at Oxford University, she counts herself as the last person to need the helping hand of a diversity scheme. Nonetheless, while at university, she spent a summer working on the Home Office 'civil service fast stream diversity internship programme'. 'Despite the many shades of brown, I'm not sure we were a "diverse" bunch', recalls Mahdawi. '[W]e were uniformly articulate and educated and hailed from pretty much the same five universities.'

A world of endless racial slights

The Equality Act 2010 provides protection against race discrimination. 'Racial grounds' include 'colour, race, nationality and ethnic and national origin'. Trades unions and advisory services take care to inform employees that discrimination can come from anywhere: 'it could be a colleague, department supervisor, your manager or your employer. Discrimination does not have to be proven as intentional — the fact that it has taken place is enough for action to be taken.'[15] The threat of action can produce an array of effects, causing employers immediately to consider the costs that a successful tribunal claim may entail, and a shadow to be cast over the workplace itself — especially when one worker is accusing another.

If internal complaints and mediation procedures fail, a race discrimination claim can be made to the UK Employment Tribunal. In 2011/12, of the 4,800 race discrimination claim applications accepted, 1,050 led to tribunal hearings and 140 were successful.[16] It is very likely that sitting behind the 4,800 applications are many more workplace race sagas that were either settled internally or eventually withdrawn.

There is no doubt that grievances are sometimes well founded and, of these, some are likely to fall foul of the vagaries of the tribunal system. But the scope for manufacturing a sense of grievance through diversity training is palpably evident. Spurious race discrimination claims not only damage the credibility of legitimate ones, but unleash a host of socially corrosive effects.[17]

In *Lofthouse v Eddie Stobart Ltd*, the case brought by Mr Lofthouse, who is mixed race, against his employer, the well-known haulage company, is laughable — and not merely because it cites the comedian Johnny Vegas. We should note at this point that, in its summary of the case, the legal website XpertHR quotes the tribunal transcript thus: '[Mr Lofthouse considers workplace banter an] important pleasure in his working life, defining it as "the mutual but jovial exchange of insults with his colleagues".'[18]

In October 2010, Mr Lofthouse alleged that he and a group of workmates were exchanging light-hearted insults whereupon he referred to an overweight colleague as 'a fat bastard like Johnny Vegas'. The colleague replied that if he was 'Johnny Vegas', Mr Lofthouse was 'the monkey' (the sock puppet from Vegas's PG Tips TV advert known as 'Monkey'). The company investigated the incident and a director apologised for the 'perceived slight', giving the offending workmates a written warning.

Mr Lofthouse's subsequent tribunal claim of race discrimination argued that his working environment was racist and a number of incidents had led to the 'unpleasant' monkey incident. His legal argument was that Eddie Stobart Ltd was 'vicariously liable' because it had handled his complaint with insufficient 'vigour'. The lack of vigour, claimed Mr Lofthouse, meant the company could not deploy the statutory defence against vicarious liability. Such a defence would require Eddie Stobart Ltd to show it had taken 'all reasonable steps' to prevent Mr Lofthouse from being likened to 'monkey'.

In the event Mr Lofthouse slipped up. His claim that the 'racist environment' meant that he was persistently called 'PG' was inconsistent with the Johnny Vegas incident to which the 'PG' banter had supposedly led up. Another earlier incident, which Mr Lofthouse *had* reported to the company (a colleague had threatened to 'rip his head off') was found by the tribunal to lack a racial connotation. The company was found to have dealt with the monkey incident 'entirely properly'.

And, indeed, the idea that any of Mr Lofthouse's claims amounted to race discrimination was a joke. But the claim could so easily have been found in Mr Lofthouse's favour. The company had been diligent in avoiding common-sense responses to the monkey incident: it had investigated the affair, invoked disciplinary proceedings against the hapless workmates and duly apologised to the wounded Mr Lofthouse. But if it hadn't taken all these excruciating steps it would have later failed to mount the all-important *statutory defence*.[19]

In other words, the 'reasonable steps' that must be shown in cases such as these are not, at the level of common sense, reasonable at all. And the eggshells that co-workers must now walk on to avoid further disciplinary proceedings come at a price — not least the 'jovial exchange of insults' Mr Lofthouse himself counted as an 'important pleasure in his working life'.

One organisation that might not have felt too pressing a need for staff diversity training was Hackney Action for Race Equality (HARE), a now-defunct advice service funded by the council. Given its role in advising on race discrimination cases, it no doubt had considerable expertise. But in 1999, Natasha Sivanandan applied for a post at HARE which included that of 'race discrimination case worker'.[20] Following an interview, Sivanandan was turned down for the post. She immediately began tribunal proceedings against both HARE and the council, alleging race and sex discrimination. Sivanandan argued that she had been treated unfairly at the interview because she had previously sued HARE following rejection at a past interview.[21]

Arguably Natasha Sivanandan was, by this time, well qualified to advise on sex and race discrimination cases.[22] According to the *Daily Telegraph*, she had launched claims against the BBC in 1992, Islington council and Barnardo's in 1996, and Enfield council and Enfield Race Equality Council in 1997.[23] In 2003, states the *Telegraph*, Sivanandan sued London Quadrant housing association for failing to move her after she complained of racist behaviour by a neighbour (she was given 'a reported £22,000 settlement and moved to a three bedroom house'). In 2009 she brought a claim against Advice for Life, a legal help charity, having lodged her first grievance there within one week of starting employment.

In 2007, eight years on from her claim, the case against HARE resulted in one of Sivanandan's interviewers being forced to pay her £1,905 for 'injury to feelings caused by race discrimination'. In 2009, HARE's funders, the council, were forced to pay out £421,415.[24] One former employee of HARE said of Sivanandan: 'She thinks the whole world is against her. She is an extremely intelligent and capable person who could have done anything she wanted...'[25]

Elisabeth Lasch-Quinn speaks of the cloying feeling of being permanently victimised by a monolithic system of white injustice, so often perceived as the underlying message of 'race experts'. But, says Lasch-Quinn, 'when we lose our ability to know when we are crying wolf and when our cries are based on real actionable injustice, the basis for claiming legitimate redress recedes'.[26] For Lasch-Quinn, the contemporary trend that reduces anti-racism to a narrow focus on etiquette and sensitivity (and legal arbitration) leaves us 'mired in a generalised sense of complaint and outrage that never seems to subside'.[27]

The contrast between Natasha Sivanandan's apparent reworking of anti-racist struggle and the conception of struggle which, in the 1960s, 70s and 80s, formed the outlook of her father, Ambalavaner Sivanandan, the veteran radical theorist and director of the Institute of Race Relations (IRR), is telling. Today's anti-racist outlook still regards racism as endemic but finds evidence of it much harder to track down. Macpherson gave credence to the belief that the trace-evidence is, in fact, all around us so long as we can be sensitive to its signs. The likes of Natasha Sivanandan offer a glimpse of how hypersensitivity, once trapped in a world — as Lasch-Quinn puts it — 'of endless slights', can reach grotesque proportions.

Despite describing his daughter's litigation spree as 'unconscionable', however, Ambalavaner Sivanandan is unlikely to ever regard Macpherson as providing the articulating principle for serial offence-seekers.[28] Meanwhile, as I write, Natasha Sivanandan, now a qualified barrister, is claiming race and sex discrimination against the Independent Police Complaints Commission (IPCC) for failing to give her an interview for a job as complaints investigator.[29]

Young, racist and white:
demonising working-class youth

As Professor Roger Hewitt describes in *White Backlash and the Politics of Multiculturalism*, the period leading up to the Macpherson Inquiry had seen a growing popular revulsion toward racist violence. In tandem with this, observes Hewitt, there grew 'a patina of middle class suspicions about a working class predisposition towards racism said to be evident in the routinely racist "canteen culture" of the Metropolitan police, and in the violence of working class adolescent "racist thugs"'.[30]

Timed to coincide with publication of the Macpherson Report, the *Daily Mirror* ran the headlines 'Into Hell' and 'Estate of Hate'.[31] The three-page story described reporter Brian Reade's journey into the Brooks Estate in Eltham, Greenwich, where he discovered 'E-reg Escort land', where race hate is 'a way of life passed down from father to son'. This, said Reade, was the 'breeding ground of four of the five men accused of stabbing Stephen Lawrence... Five products of a twisted philosophy drummed into them from birth'. Yet, implied Reade, such endemic racism was everywhere: 'who among us can say Eltham is radically different from parts of our own towns or cities?'[32]

The *Mirror* was far from alone in its re-awakening of such prejudices. Hewitt sums up the post-Macpherson prejudice towards sections of the white working class, a group frequently dubbed the 'British underclass': 'the message was that in looking for racism in the UK there was no need to look further.'[33]

As Hewitt observes, the contempt exuding from the media merely intensified white, working-class resentment that had been smouldering for years. In south-east London, much of this resentment could be attributed to official anti-racist policies. From 1986, Greenwich Council chose to retain the outgoing Inner London Education Authority's (ILEA) commitment to multiculturalism and anti-racism. By the time Macpherson was recommending that the nation's schools record and report all 'racist incidents', Greenwich had been doing it for years.[34] In Hewitt's study, the majority of young white people interviewed on certain Greenwich estates in the early 1990s were of the opinion that schools favoured black pupils. The determination with which schools carried out 'racist incident' recording policies paid little heed to their corrosive impact on the ground.

Hewitt quotes one youth worker's description of the resentment felt by white youth when caught up in school fights with black or Asian kids: 'straightaway it's deemed [by the school] as a racist attack. It becomes a much more serious incident because race is involved and from their point of view it's not always a race issue... And they carry that with them and now the anger is... in a sense it's caused racism because they've carried that unfairness with them.'[35] Another youth worker told Hewitt: 'when they talk about white people having all the power, well the young people I work with haven't. They don't have any power at all.' As Hewitt notes, 'they saw themselves as also constituting an aggrieved minority and there was considerable evidence that, indeed, they were'.[36]

If this was the picture in the years leading up to the Macpherson Inquiry, it was nothing compared to the years that followed Brian Reade's 'estate of hate' condemnation.

Veteran anti-racist and community worker Dev Barrah has witnessed the decline in racism within Greenwich. In 2008 I interviewed Barrah for my 2009 report *The Myth of Racist Kids*.[37] Kenyan-born Barrah, one of many experts consulted by the Macpherson Inquiry, refuses to join in the demonising of the white working-class residents of the local estates. These are his neighbourhoods, and his people—'so many brilliant people'.

Barrah is contemptuous of the idea that a virulent racism resides and ferments in white-dominated, working-class areas like Eltham and Abbey Wood. The difference today compared to the past, he observes, is that incidents are less frequent, but are taken far more seriously. He laments the way the media still delights in describing Eltham as the 'racist capital' of Britain: in reality, incidents are rare, often name-calling and invariably committed by 'the usual suspects'. As we talked, Barrah recalled 'the last incident in Eltham', which took place three weeks previously: 'And that was when someone drove past in a car

and shouted "nigger" at [a woman] and she recognised him—
she knows him from when he was little. When I checked the
BNP list he was on there!'[38]

Barrah's work in one part of the borough showed that the
'racist' incidents leading to this neighbourhood being flagged
up as a 'hotspot' could be largely traced to two families. Both
had teenage boys engaged in anti-social behaviour and petty
crime, and these boys were as big a problem to their white
neighbours as they were to anyone else. Barrah and his team
knocked on every door in this supposed 'hotspot'. White people
were as concerned about the activities of these boys as anybody
else. A well-attended public meeting discussed the harassment
of non-white residents, and attributed this to the antisocial
behaviour of a few.[39]

In 2011, an evaluation report for a major four-year-long anti-
racism project in Greenwich, Bexley and Barking & Dagenham
began with: 'Racist violence continues to be a serious problem in
Britain.'[40] It then stated: 'In 2010/11 more than 51,187 racist
incidents were recorded by the police in England and Wales…
The British Crime Survey estimates that the actual number of
such incidents is around 200,000 annually.'[41] The report's evalu-
ators, headed by none other than the Macpherson Inquiry's pre-
eminent expert Dr Robin Oakley, summarise the anti-racism
project as a fresh alternative to current approaches ('responding
to incidents once they have occurred is too limited an
approach').[42] What is needed, they say, is 'a more proactive
response that draws out the problem and confronts it with the
aim of prevention…'.[43]

The 'problem' motivating this anti-racist intervention was, it
seems, that of young, white males imagined as '*potential* perpetrators of racist violence' (my emphasis).[44] Significant here is
the roll-out of the post-Macpherson legislation, with its general
duty to have 'due regard' to the need to eliminate discrimination, which is frequently translated as entailing the need to take
urgent action on racist incidents *before they occur*. It is also
significant how incident statistics are presented as the impera-
tive for action despite the fact that they have been largely

generated from 'hate crimes' based on Macpherson's emphasis on the *perception* of racism.

The Stephen Lawrence case is proudly noted by the evaluation report as having 'brought Greenwich and its neighbouring boroughs to national and international attention as a *cauldron for racist violence*' (my emphasis).[45] By citing brutal racist murder and violence, the evaluation report constructs a vision of east and south-east London as a breeding ground for potential perpetrators.[46] In its first 20 pages alone, the apparent influence of the far right on London's white, working-class male population is mentioned 13 times (either as 'the far right', 'extremist political groups', 'the British National Party (BNP)' or 'the English Defence League (EDL)').

Curiously, the nuanced research work of Roger Hewitt, author of *White Backlash and the Politics of Multiculturalism*, is cited approvingly as affirming the project workers' view that 'any young people could be potential perpetrators of racist violence', and that 'rather than trying to single individuals out, it is necessary to work more broadly with young people around racial and identity issues'.[47]

Doubtless the frequency with which working-class youth violently clash with one another is quite high. But the nature of such conflict is multi-varied — sometimes it generates from petty territorial fights centred on housing estates; often it is street robbery. By racialising these issues and creating a generalised phenomenon of white, racist violence, the reality of what is actually happening on the ground becomes skewed. On this question, Oakley's evaluation report only hints that the picture might be more complicated. In passing, the report mentions work carried out with Year 9 African boys who, in the words of a project worker, 'have admitted carrying out several violent and unprovoked attacks on innocent members of the public'.

The Greenwich project, we are told, began with its project worker consulting 'professional colleagues in the youth work field': '[S]ome were very engaged with issues of racism in the Greenwich area, whereas others felt this was no longer such an important issue and wanted to put the history of past events behind them and move on.'[48] A preliminary report on the Greenwich project was presented to various local agencies for comment (including youth service managers, a school, the 'safer neighbourhoods panel'). Not all comments were positive. Some responses appeared, say Oakley *et al.*, '...to be fairly negative, apparently because they felt that it was exaggerating or amplifying a problem that didn't really exist...'.[49]

My filmmaking has frequently centred on work in Greenwich and Lewisham, with refugee and asylum seeker youth. They came from Somalia, Sierra Leone, Vietnam, Bosnia, Afghanistan, Roma communities in eastern Europe... and most had now lived in south London for several years. A typical schools project in 2001 had ended in a film called *Safe*, a short documentary about the experiences of five asylum seeker teenagers living in London.[50]

Their accounts of life at crumbling Malory School and on the streets of the impoverished estates that surrounded it did not mention racism: this was a concept they were more likely to associate with the countries from which they had fled. The kids in *Safe* simply wanted to talk about the constant risk of being 'rushed' (mugged) on the streets of south London, an experience that would usually entail their mobile phones being grabbed from them but would sometimes involve being cut with knives.

No off switch:
the divisive logic of multiculturalist policies

The violent disturbances in northern English towns in the summer of 2001 sparked a confused narrative about apparent failures in multiculturalist policy that continues to this day. A Home Office report into the disorder that swept through Bradford and Oldham seemed startled to find that many ethnic communities 'operate on the basis of a series of parallel lives'.[51] 'These lives often do not seem to touch at any point let alone overlap and promote meaningful interchanges', observed Ted Cantle, who chaired the group that wrote the report. Cantle went on to argue that entrenched divisions were caused by ethnically-based state funding encouraging groups to compete against each other. The report further argued that these divisions were compounded by 'our anxiety to eliminate forms of insulting behaviour and language', leading to an unwilling-ness 'to open any subject which might possibly lead to uncom-fortable differences in opinion'.[52]

The Cantle Report had rightly identified the destructive trend inherent within diversity policies. However, from the moment it was published in December 2001, these observations amounted to whistling in the wind. The Macpherson Report, and specifically its theory of 'institutional racism', had already institutionalised the politics of difference. Its power and purpose drowned out Cantle's words—there was no off switch.

The riots that had swept British cities in 1981 were a product of racism, both in the police and across society. By contrast, the 2001 riots that Ted Cantle had sought to explain were the product of municipal anti-racism and its multicultural funding strategies. These had laid down divisive, racial fault lines and nurtured intractable conflicts and rivalries which otherwise insignificant groups like the BNP could all too easily exploit. In the wake of the 2001 riots, BNP leader Nick Griffin was inter-viewed on BBC's *Newsnight*, where he simply followed the logic of multiculturalism: Asians are not inferior to whites, argued Griffin, it is just that their culture, values and lifestyle are *too different* from white culture.[53]

Just three years later, in Birmingham, another riot would erupt. Intractable conflicts and rivalries with Asians were cited here too: 'If you want a taxi—Asian. If you want petrol—Asian. Off-licence—Asian. Access to banks—Asian… Our community feels trapped.'[54] But these were the words of the respected anti-racist, Maxie Hayles, who had been a respondent to the Macpherson Inquiry.[55]

Birmingham's Lozells riots brought the pernicious, divisive character of multiculturalism and anti-racism into even sharper relief. These were dubbed 'race riots', rather like the Handsworth riots 10 years earlier, except this time the pitched battles were not with the police: they were between black and

Asian youth. For two days in October 2005, they fought each other. On the first evening of the riot, walking home through Lozells, 23-year-old Isiah Young-Sam was attacked and stabbed to death by a gang of Asian men ostensibly because he was black.[56]

The trigger for the riots had been a rumour. Stories had circulated that a black girl had been gang-raped by Asian men. The police investigation found nothing to substantiate this rumour,[57] but it escalated via local black radio DJs who called for a large demonstration in protest. DJ Warren G, who had described the rape rumour on-air, would later learn of the death of his school friend, Isiah Young-Sam. One phone-in caller to Sting FM said, 'there are not enough of you pussies out there in the street! This is between blacks and Pakis'.[58] African-Caribbean community leaders added their own calls for a boycott of Asian shops.

The demonstrations that followed turned quickly into rioting. African-Caribbeans later claimed Asian gangs had attacked the demo shouting 'kill the niggers'; Asians claimed the black demonstrators had attacked their shops with baseball bats and bricks.[59]

A rumour may have sparked the violence — but a tinderbox of accumulated grievance lent it an additional fury. The black, predominantly working-class, residents of Birmingham had, for decades, built up resentment towards their Asian neighbours. 'Blacks get nothing, no funding, no support', said one African-Caribbean community worker after the riots. 'Blacks make Asians rich, we support their shops. It's a joke.'[60] Respected community leaders joined in. 'We have a South African situation here', said Maxi Hayles of the Birmingham Racial Attack Monitoring Unit. 'White on top, coloured Asian in the middle and African at the bottom… the fact is the Afro-Caribbeans were here first, then the Asians came.'[61] The Asian residents of Birmingham held their own grievances. 'They come into our shops, but can't stop stealing. Niggers can't help it', 26-year-old Makaveli told the *Guardian*. 'They have a dirty gene. They are the lowest of the low.'[62]

For community leaders on both sides, the grievances sounded much the same — that the council always treated one group better than the other. Kenan Malik's account of what lay at the heart of this is worth summarising.[63] The answer lies, says Malik, in the city's multiculturalist policies installed after the 1985 Handsworth riots. Birmingham City Council had followed the GLC's example by sponsoring new 'community' groups based on ethnicity and faith. This was intended to foster representation of specific group needs, help the council allocate funding and ensure good 'race relations'.

The new community groups proliferated. They included the Bangledeshi Islamic Projects Consultative Committee, the Council for Black-led Churches, the Pakistani Forum, the African and Caribbean People's Movement and many more. The glaring irony of this 'diversity' policy was its divisive effect. So-called community 'leaders' (they had no local mandate) jostled to claim the right to speak up for the needs of 'their' community. Worse still, Asian and Black groups became pitted against one another as they compete for a share of state resources.[64]

Birmingham's multiculturalist solution, comments Malik, 'did not respond to the needs of communities, but to a large degree *created* those communities by imposing identities on people'. Class conflicts, for example, were erased from the picture. 'Once political power and financial resources became allocated by ethnicity,' observes Malik, 'then people began to identify themselves in terms of their ethnicity, and *only* their ethnicity.'[65]

Racialised identities, and their associated rifts and sensitivities, cultivated by policies designed to enhance 'race relations', smouldered onward. Old scores rose to the surface. The resentment felt by Birmingham's black population toward Asians took an increasingly hostile form. Just months after the 2005 Lozells riot, Malik found very few of Birmingham's African-Caribbean leaders willing to be interviewed for his Channel 4 film. One of the few who participated was Anthony Gordon, chair of the Partnership Against Crime; before the interview, Gordon demanded that Malik account for what he viewed as the crimes of the Asian community.

Malik told Gordon that he could only speak for himself, not all Asians. 'But Asians have always had it in for the black man. It was like that in South Africa. It was like that in Kenya and Uganda. And it's like that here. It's in your blood', replied Gordon. Reflecting on this encounter, Malik points to, not the 'black-on-Asian' racism visible at the surface, but rather the divisive politics at its root: 'Hostility is not in the blood of Asians or African-Caribbeans. It is in the DNA of multicultural policies.'[66]

From 1999 onwards, the Macpherson effect — its institution-alisation of the divisive politics of difference — could only have hardened the racial thinking that ignited the Lozells conflict. Today, official anti-racism and multiculturalism are indis-tinguishable. At their centre is the elevation of ethnic and religious identity, framed by the overarching identity of *victim*. As a consequence, policy serves merely to unleash petty squabbles over status and resources, with rival groups com-peting for a higher position in a hierarchy of grievance. Modern anti-racism serves to intensify a sense of victimhood further, by exaggerating the everyday presence of racism. This, in turn, encourages individual members of ethnic minorities to racialise adverse experiences, regardless of their root cause.[67]

With grievance established as both a virtue and a way of making certain demands, the results are frequently grotesque and a far cry from anything anti-racists have in mind. When Maxi Hayles voiced his contempt for Asians he veered dramatically off-script. Yet all he had really done was follow the logic of identity politics. This had been officially acceptable when he had been talking to the Macpherson Inquiry about the racism inflicted on his 'community' by white society,[68] but now his ire had simply moved to another perceived oppressor — 'the Asians'.

The same elevation of racial identity and concomitant group injury had propelled both sides in the Lozells riots. For white, working-class youth in Greenwich, claiming their own version of racial victimhood also feels like a logical step – especially when faced with the accusing stereotype which casts all of them as either racists or potential racists. And the same cloying sense of personal and group 'racial' sensitivity – further cultivated by diversity training and grievance procedures – acts as the driver for numerous damaging and fruitless discrimination tribunals. 'Hypersensitivity', says the American writer Elizabeth Lasch-Quinn, 'makes for thinner and thinner skins.'

Moreover, the era of anti-racism – be it with formal manifestations like diversity training or just the sense in which the rules of racial etiquette float in the cultural ether – has meant that, to paraphrase Kenan Malik, the *fear* of giving racial offence has made it far easier to *take* offence.[69] Flushed with the certainty that human interaction is riddled with 'unwitting' slights and injured feelings, anti-racism unleashes division and estrangement and conflict. Viewed, first, through the prism of race-identity, our everyday encounters then become defined not by our actions or words or good intentions but by assumptions over what might be unwitting and unconscious that we have contracted from the culture around us.

As the writer Bruno Waterfield observed of 'the Macpherson effect' in 2003, freedom is thrown into question, as '…nothing can be shared. We have nothing in common, it seems; we need the guidance of former judges like Sir William Macpherson, who are somehow able to stand above the cultural pressures that transform mere mortals into unwitting racists'.[70]

'What is really dangerous is when you don't know that you've censored yourself', commented the author Monica Ali.[71] In our re-working of Orwell, a true 'goodthinker' is someone who never needs to self-censor; they have conformed to the rules and can simply scan the world around them for error. The rest must keep their radars discreetly turned upon themselves.

Endnotes:

1   Malik, K. (2007) 'Thinking Outside the Box', *Catalyst*, Jan–Feb. Accessed 11 June 2014. Available at: http://www.kenanmalik.com/

essays/catalyst_box.html

2   Gillborn, D. (2008) *Racism and Education, Coincidence or Conspiracy?*,
     London: Routledge, p27.

3   Malik, K. (2013) 'The Pleasures of Pluralism, the Pain of Offence',
     Pandemonium, 17 June. Accessed 20 May 2014. Available at: http://
     kenanmalik.wordpress.com/2013/06/17/the-pleasures-of-pluralism
     -the-pain-of-offence/

4   In *Nineteen Eighty-Four* Orwell speaks of 'the B vocabulary' — a list of
     words 'intended to impose a desirable mental attitude upon the per-
     son using them'. 'The Party told you to reject the evidence of your
     senses. It was their final, most essential command.' See: Orwell, G.
     (1949) *Nineteen Eighty-Four*, London: Twentieth Century Classics,
     1974, Appendix p84 and p216; also cited in Dennis, N., Erdos, G.,
     and Al-Shahi, A. (2000) *Racist Murder and Pressure Group Politics: The
     Macpherson Report and the Police*, London: Civitas, p106, in which the
     authors note 'The goodthinker will in all circumstances know, with-
     out taking thought, what is true belief about what the facts are, and
     desirable emotion in response to them'.

5   See: Macpherson, W. (1999) *The Stephen Lawrence Inquiry*, UK
     Government Command Paper 4262–1, Ch 47.39. Recommendation
     39 states: 'That consideration should be given to amendment of the
     law to allow prosecution of offences involving racist language or
     behaviour, and of offences involving the possession of offensive
     weapons, where such conduct can be proved to have taken place
     otherwise than in a public place.'

6   Duodi, C. (2006) 'I'm Not Racist But… How could a judge not realise
     the seriousness of playground abuse?', *Guardian*, 10 April. Accessed
     20 May 2014. Available at: http://www.theguardian.com/
     commentisfree/2006/apr/10/cameronduodunooneisracist

7   Macpherson, W. (1999) *Op. cit.*, Ch 7.42.

8   Brown, B. (2001) *Combating Discrimination: Persona Dolls in Action*,
     Stoke-on-Trent: Trentham Books, p39. NB: EYTARN contributed to
     the Macpherson Inquiry.

9   *Ibid.*, p38.

10   Furedi, F. (2011) *On Tolerance: A Defence of Moral Independence*,
     London: Continuum, pp70–71.

11   Mahdawi, A. (2012) 'I'm Not Racist, Some of My Colleagues are
     White — What is "Diversity" Anyway?', *Guardian*, 15 March 2012.
     Accessed 14 May 2014. Available at: http://www.theguardian.com/
     commentisfree/2012/mar/15/diversity-social-mobility-harvard-
     business-review

12   Bregman, P. (2012) 'Diversity Training Doesn't Work', *Psychology
     Today*, 12 March. Accessed 14 May 2014. Available at: http://www.
     psychologytoday.com/blog/how-we-work/201203/diversity-
     training-doesnt-work

[13]   Lasch-Quinn, E. (2001) *Race Experts: How Racial Etiquette, Sensitivity Training, and New Age Therapy Hijacked the Civil Rights Movement,* New York: Norton, pxviii.

[14]   See: Judge, T.A., and Cable, D.M. (2011) 'When It Comes to Pay, Do the Thin Win? The Effect of Weight on Pay for Men and Women', *Journal of Applied Psychology,* 96(1), pp95–112. Accessed 18 May 2014. Available at: http://www.timothy-judge.com/Judge%20and%20 Cable%20(JAP%202010).pdf

[15]   See: Citizens Advice Bureau online advice guide. Accessed 14 May 2014. Available at: http://www.adviceguide.org.uk/nireland/ work_ni/faq_index_employment/faq_employment_racial_discrimi nation_at_work.htm

[16]   Ministry of Justice (2012) 'Employment Tribunals and EAT Statistics', 20 September, London: HMSO. Accessed on 11 June 2014. Available at: https://www.gov.uk/government/uploads/system/ uploads/attachment_data/file/218497/employment-trib-stats-april-march-2011-12.pdf

[17]   *Personnel Today* (2000) 'New Laws Blamed as Major Factor in Claims to Tribunals'. Accessed 20 May 2014. Available at: http://www. personneltoday.com/hr/new-laws-blamed-as-major-factor-in-claims-to-tribunals/

[18]   The case is summarised by the legal website XpertHR. See: 'Mixed Race Employee Called "the Monkey" Loses Discrimination Claim.' Accessed 14 May 2014. Available at: http://www.xperthr.co.uk/ editors-choice/mixed-race-employee-called-the-monkey-loses-discrimination-claim/112043/. NB: Soon after the 'monkey' incident Eddie Stobart Ltd dismissed MR Lofthouse for an unrelated incident involving health and safety. Eventually Mr Lofthouse was reinstated. It was at this point that he brought a race discrimination claim forward. See: http://businessdatabase.indicator.co.uk/ business_advice_directory/articles/discrimination/avoiding_ liability_in_discrimination_claims/UKTAPSAR_EU140702?q=. Accessed 15 July 2014.

[19]   Organisations are likely to introduce Diversity Training in anticipation of possible tribunal claims so that a commitment to good interpersonal relations can be demonstrated. The inescapable irony here is that the training has the capacity to stir grievance and resentment... and tribunal claims. For some workforces it must surely be doomed from the start. Diversity Training is mercilessly lampooned by Tommy Gavin (played by Denis Leary) in the US TV show *Rescue Me* (2005), season 2, episode 5. See: http://www.youtube.com/ watch?v=egAMgNY84do. Accessed 14 June 2014.

[20]   Edwards, A. (2013) 'Race Equality Adviser Awarded £420,000 by Tribunal Judges because She was Turned Down for a Council-Funded Job 14 YEARS AGO', *Daily Mail,* 30 January. Accessed 20

May 2014. Available at: http://www.dailymail.co.uk/news/article-2270535/Race-equality-advisor-handed-400k-court-victimisation-group-refused-job.html

21   Leach, B. (2011) 'Million-Pound Bill for Taxpayer After Race Activist Sues Anti-Racism Groups', *Daily Telegraph*, 11 June. Accessed 15 May 2014. Available at: http://www.telegraph.co.uk/news/uknews/law-and-order/8569956/Million-pound-bill-for-taxpayer-after-race-activist-sues-anti-racism-groups.html

22   *Ibid.* The *Daily Telegraph* also points out that Sivanandan later 'qualified as a barrister in October 2006'.

23   *Ibid.*

24   *Daily Telegraph* (2013) 'Judge Says £420,000 Racism Claim Can Stand, After 13 Years of "Dickensian" Wrangling', *Daily Telegraph*, 29 January. Accessed 20 May 2014. Available at: http://www.telegraph.co.uk/news/uknews/law-and-order/9834316/Judge-says-420000-racism-claim-can-stand-after-13-years-of-Dickensian-wrangling.html

25   Leach, B. (2011) *Op. cit.* Leach reports that HARE 'ceased operating partly as a result of her action'.

26   Lasch-Quinn, E. (2001) *Race Experts: How Racial Etiquette, Sensitivity Training, and New Age Therapy Hijacked the Civil Rights Movement*, New York: Norton, pxvii.

27   *Ibid.*, pxviii.

28   See: Leach, B. (2011) *Op. cit.* Ambalavaner Sivanandan is quoted: 'It goes against the basic rules of fairness and natural justice. Irrespective of whether or not she is my daughter I believe her actions have been unconscionable… She has taken money directly from the organisations I have fought to help throughout my career.'

29   See: Qureshi, Y. (2013) 'Barrister to Sue Police for "Failing to Give Her a Job Interview"', *Manchester Evening News*, 2 December.

30   Hewitt, R. (2005) *White Backlash and the Politics of Multiculturalism*, Cambridge: Cambridge University Press, p52.

31   Reade, B. (1999) 'REPORT TO SHAME BRITAIN: ESTATE OF HATE; Brian Reade walks the streets where racism is a way of life – and death. He finds that even the young have been poisoned', *Daily Mirror*, 24 February. Accessed 20 May 2014. Available at: http://www.thefreelibrary.com/REPORT+TO+SHAME+BRITAIN%3A+ESTATE+OF+HATE%3B+Brian+Reade+walks+the...-a060397694. This article is also cited by Hewitt (2005), p53.

32   *Ibid.*

33   Hewitt, R. (2005) *Op. cit.*, p53. Hewitt notes how the theme of 'underclass' had been developed for some time in the *Sunday Times* with the help of academic Charles Murray.

34   *Ibid.*, p122.

35   *Ibid.*, p123.

36   *Ibid.*, p124.
37   Hart, A. (2009) *The Myth of Racist Kids: Anti-Racist Policy and the Regulation of School Life,* London: The Manifesto Club, p32.
38   The BNP membership 'list', leaked in 2009, is unimpressive. In Greenwich and Lewisham (with a combined population of 478,000), 66 residents were listed as past or present members. See: http://wikileaks.org/wiki/British_National_Party_membership_list_and_other_information%2C_15_Apr_2009
39   Hart, A. (2009) *Op. cit.*, p33.
40   Oakley, R., Isal, S., and Woods, A. (2011) *Are You Saying I'm a Racist? An Evaluation of Work to Tackle Racist Violence in Three Areas of London,* Trust for London, p5.
41   See: Ministry of Justice (2011) 'Statistics on Race and the Criminal Justice System'. Accessed 16 May 2014. Available at: https://www.gov.uk/government/uploads/system/uploads/attachment_data/file/219967/stats-race-cjs-2010.pdf

     Here, the Home Office document (and source of the police 51,187 and 9464 'racist incident' figures and the BCS figure) reminds us that the police use the Macpherson definition and that 'Research from across England and Wales indicates that the majority of racist incidents recorded involve either damage to property or verbal harassment'. It points out that the England and Wales figure for 2010/11 of 51,187 had fallen significantly: '…a decrease of almost 18% across the last five years (2006/07 to 2010/11).' Moreover, one of the largest falls had been London. The BCS is 'a large-scale nationally representative survey that asks people aged 16 or over about their experience of crime in the last 12 months'. Its figure of 150,000 (rounded up to 200,000 by the Trust for London project evaluators) should be viewed alongside the figure of '9,618,000 incidents of crime overall', but also alongside the fact that the survey sample group is invited to volunteer instances of racially motivated crime based on the Macpherson definition: 'any criminal offence which is perceived, by the victim or any other person, to be motivated by a hostility or prejudice towards someone based on a personal characteristic' (in this case, 'race').
42   Oakley, R., Isal, S., and Woods, A. (2011) *Are You Saying I'm a Racist? An Evaluation of Work to Tackle Racist Violence in Three Areas of London,* Trust for London, p4. 'Unless a new approach is taken we can expect to stay in the present malaise of racial malaise of racial conflict which blights many communities and remains unchanged', concludes the report's foreword, by the Venerable Peter Delaney MBE, Vice-Chair of the Trust for London.
43   *Ibid.*, p5. Note: the background to this intervention by Trust for London had been a 2005 Runnymede Trust report: *Preventing Racist Violence – Work with Actual and Potential Perpetrators.*

44   *Ibid.,* p11.

45   *Ibid.,* p16.

46   *Ibid.,* p16. Alongside the Lawrence murder, those of Rohit Duggal
      and Rolan Adams are cited. The report does concede, however, that
      'Community opinion remains divided between those who feel that
      racism [over 20 years later] remains a serious issue in the borough
      [of Greenwich], and those who feel the situation is much improved
      and that it is time to put the history to one side and move on'.

47   *Ibid.,* p13.

48   *Ibid.,* p18.

49   *Ibid.,* p19.

50   The film *Safe* went on to win the London Weekend Television (LWT)
      'Whose London' competition in 2001, broadcast the following year.
      The film's success was a testament to the participating students who
      devised, shot and starred in the film with the help of Stella Barnes
      and myself. At that time Stella Barnes was at the forefront (along
      with Adam A. Annand, Yolande Baptiste and others) of innovative,
      participatory — and frankly extraordinary — work, carried out by
      Greenwich and Lewisham Young People's Theatre (GLYPT) under
      the direction of the late Viv Harris.

51   Cantle, T. (2001) *Community Cohesion: A Report of the Independent
      Review Team Chaired by Ted Cantle,* London: Home Office.

52   *Ibid.*

53   The *Newsnight* example is cited by Kenan Malik's (2001) talk 'The
      Changing Meaning of Race'. Accessed 20 May 2014. Available at:
      http://www.kenanmalik.com/lectures/race_oxford1_print.html

54   Vulliamy, E. (2005) 'Rumours of a Riot', *Guardian,* 29 November.
      Accessed 16 May 2014. Available at: http://www.theguardian.com/
      uk/2005/nov/29/race.world

55   Part 2 of the Macpherson Inquiry visited Birmingham on 13
      November 1998 ('Day 11').

56   *Guardian* (2006) 'Race Riot Killers Jailed for Life', 22 May. Accessed
      20 May 2014. Available at: http://www.theguardian.com/uk/2006/
      may/22/ukcrime.race

57   Townsend, M. (2005) 'The New Colour of British Racism', *Guardian,*
      30 October. Accessed 16 May 2014. Available at: http://www.
      theguardian.com/uk/2005/oct/30/race.world
          Townsend writes: 'Despite a police investigation finding no
      evidence of the rape, the black community is adamant it is true. In
      turn, the Asian community believes the "rape" was conceived as an
      excuse to attack their shops.'

58   Malik, K. (2009) *From Fatwa to Jihad: The Rushdie Affair and its Legacy,*
      London: Atlantic Books, p64.

59   Vulliamy, E. (2005) *Op. cit.*

60   Appleton, J. (2005) 'What's Behind the Battle of Lozells?', *Spiked,* 26

October. Accessed 21 May 2014. Available at:http://www.spiked-online.com/newsite/article/506#.U3YXxIFdXfI

[61] Vulliamy, E. (2005) *Op. cit.*

[62] Townsend, M. (2005) *Op. cit.*

[63] Malik, K. (2009) *Op. cit.,* pp63–9.

[64] *Ibid.,* p68.

[65] *Ibid.,* pp67–8.

[66] *Ibid.,* p71.

[67] Fitzpatrick, M. (2005) 'The Price of Multiculturalism', *Spiked,* 5 August. Accessed 20 May 2014. Available at: http://www.spiked-online.com/newsite/article/694#.U3s2z9JdXfI

[68] Hayles's view, related to Macpherson, was that community groups like his own (BRAMU) stood on the front line of fighting racism both in the sense of monitoring violent attacks (and supporting victims) and railing against the institutional racism of Birmingham City Council as evidenced by its failure to fund BRAMU adequately. Ten years on, his view of society is not much changed: 'Few will call you a black bastard but we all saw the list of BNP people. It's about attitude. We know it's there.' In the same *Guardian* article youth worker Leroy McKoy makes a very different point: '[McKoy] tells local teenagers about police hostility and racial conflict in the 1970s. But it is just a history lesson for the boys, for they say they have black friends, white friends, Asian friends, Somalian friends.' See: Muir, H. (2009) 'In Macpherson's Footsteps: A Journey Through British Racism', *Guardian,* 21 February. Accessed 20 May 2014. Available at: http://www.theguardian.com/uk/2009/feb/21/stephen-lawrence-racism-macpherson-report. See also transcripts from the Macpherson Inquiry (Part 2, Day 11, p120) posted by Dr Richard Stone on his blog. Accessed on 11 June 2014. Available at: http://richardstonesli.files.wordpress.com/2012/02/d011slp2.pdf

[69] Malik, K. (2009) *Op. cit.,* p196.

[70] Waterfield, B. (2003) 'Imposing "Parallel Lives"', *Spiked,* 22 January. Accessed 20 May 2014. Available at: http://www.spiked-online.com/newsite/article/6811#.U3YiWIFdXfI

[71] Malik, K. (2009) *Op. cit.,* p197.

Chapter Four

The Myth of Racist Kids

The publication, in 2009, of *The Myth of Racist Kids* instantly triggered a brusque response. My conclusions were 'unacceptable', said Chris Keates, General Secretary of the teachers' union NASUWT in a press release.[1] 'To seek to dismiss racist taunts as "playground spats" shows a breathtaking degree of ignorance and irresponsibility', she argued; and in fact, 'the report should be expressing deep concern about the number of racist incidents recorded, not seeking to divert attention from them'.

Schools minister Diana Johnson said, 'If racist bullying is not dealt with in schools, then this will send a powerful message to children that racism is acceptable — not only in schools but in society as a whole'.[2] ITN's *More 4 News* had prepared an item in readiness for the launch of *The Myth of Racist Kids*. It drew on figures for 'violent' racist incidents and placed these alongside what they regarded as the outlandish claim made by my press release that 'the notion of racist kids is in large part a myth'.

The accusations of ignorance and irresponsibility, of trivialising the seriousness of the problem and placing children at risk of receiving the 'wrong message', offer some indication of the heresy I had allegedly committed. In fact, *The Myth of Racist Kids* had made it abundantly clear that the issue under scrutiny was the *obligation* on teachers to hunt down racist incidents in accordance with government guidelines. Instead of being free to exercise their own professional judgment about behaviour, teachers had no choice but to relinquish their authority and comply with official procedure. With the government advising teachers to record anything that anyone might perceive to be racist, it was unsurprising that name-calling, along the lines of 'chocolate bar', 'white trash' and 'blackie', became typical incidents.[3]

Worse still, the official guidelines stated: 'Failure to investigate, even where an incident appears to be of a relatively minor nature, could be seen as condoning racism and could be used as evidence that a school is not taking seriously its legal duties under the Race Relations (Amendment) Act.'[4] In other words, a good school was one in which racist incidents, however trivial, were reported to the local authority on a regular basis. As one teacher described the policy: 'You might think it's daft, you might even wonder if you're racist to think it's daft, but in any case these days you're going to think, hang on I'd better be careful here. The best thing to do is just report it.'[5]

Far from arguing that insulting behaviour should be uniformly ignored by schools, *The Myth of Racist Kids* recommended that adults exercised their authority in managing children's behaviour, but that they did not *racialise* children's relationships when doing so. It also stressed the importance of unsupervised play: 'schools should and frequently do discipline children for name-calling and bullying, just as for any other form of anti-social behaviour. But the fact that children are required to respect adult authority in the classroom does not alter their need to engage—at break-time—in unfettered peer interaction. In this sphere adults should take a step back and allow children the freedom to flourish.'[6]

What was so telling in the reactions to this argument, from a government minister, union leader and national news programme, was their assumption that the state's bureaucratic management of racist incident reporting was the only trustworthy approach to the problem. Moreover, *the problem* (for which we must have 'deep concern') was conceived as something simultaneously uncovered and dealt with by the example-setting practice of official incident reporting. My contention in the report, and arguably the real reason it caused outrage, was that the notion that Britain is a deeply racist society—which, supposedly, entails a problem of racist kids—is itself a myth, with each of these presumed problems used to infer the existence of the other. In other words, the idea of an epidemic of 'racist incidents' that must be uncovered and dealt with was a self-fulfilling prophecy, conjured from the drive to record and report ever-higher figures.

Previous chapters have looked at the myth of racist Britain. In this chapter two more myths, similarly embedded in the anti-racist outlook that dominates today, need investigation. The first hinges on the belief that 'white' children are the inevitable bearers of racist attitudes (which therefore require urgent anti-racist intervention). The second sits, somewhat awkwardly, with a widespread recognition that children are, on the whole, very resilient. Because here, black and other minority non-white children are presumed, en masse, to be uniquely vulnerable to the ideas and expressions around them.

'Nipping it in the bud': the myth of 'early years racism'

The official 'race relations' rationale driving incident reporting places a particular emphasis on schools being seen to be ever-vigilant; sending out 'the right message'; and displaying, at all times, a clear 'zero tolerance' approach. In the wake of the Macpherson Report, the prospect of state-maintained schools failing to keep vigil and therefore appearing indifferent to 'racist' bullying or banter has doubtless focused the mind of many a government official not otherwise known for their commitment to anti-racism. But where did this glib one-liner, favoured by politicians and officials, that 'we must nip it in the bud' come from?

Theories about the importance of anti-racist intervention in the early years have been around for some time, and lend, at least at first glance, substance to policy in this area. A written submission from the Early Years Trainers Anti-Racist Network (EYTARN) formed part of the expertise reviewed by the Macpherson Inquiry.[7] Writing in 2001, EYTARN founder

Babette Brown cites the Macpherson Report's emphasis on how racism 'starts amongst the very young' and is 'deeply ingrained'.[8]

The Macpherson Inquiry's view, and one quite possibly influenced by EYTARN, is, claims Brown, backed up by research originally conducted in the early 1970s, which 'found that by the time they were 2 years old children noticed differences in skin colour and that by 3 and 5 they have learnt from the world around them that it is "better" to be White in Britain than Black'.[9] This research involved an experiment where children's preference for either black or white dolls appeared to correlate with racism in adult society. It echoed similar child 'doll preference' experimentation in the USA in 1947.[10]

The fact that past generations of children might have been influenced by racism in the adult world is unsurprising. Today, we would expect those influences to be considerably less. But neither of these facts have much bearing on results emanating from science-lab experiments. At any time between 1947 and now, the 'doll preference' results can differ: for example, in 1969, Hraba and Grant replicated the 1947 experiment, and found that the majority of black children aged 3 to 8 preferred a black doll and this preference increased with age.[11] A child's doll preference offers no indication of whether the child takes account of race in everyday social interactions: it requires a racialised explanation to conflate a child's acceptance of one doll with rejection of the other.

For decades, the assumption that 'doll preference experiments' reveal the hidden hand of racism has animated the doctrine of early years anti-racism. But can the complexities of child development be so easily reduced to 'evidence' that children become racist in the nursery? According to this viewpoint, the child is imagined, not as a pre-adult furiously engaged in the business of childhood, but as a hapless product of social conditioning. Anti-racists propose, as a solution, an alternative model of social conditioning. 'As individuals we cannot make the world free of racism and a safe place to be', says Jane Lane, author of the 366-page training manual *Young Children and*

*Racial Justice: Taking action for racial equality in the early years –
understanding the past, thinking about the present, planning for the
future*, published in 2008 by the National Children's Bureau
(NCB). '[B]ut we can do our very best to ensure that our early
years settings are small models of what we would like the
world to be.'[12]

It can be assumed that, for Lane, 'we' means early years
workers liberated from the scourge of racist conditioning by
recourse to training. Her opening claim – 'Young children are
sponges' – is emphasised in the Foreword, written by Herman
Ouseley, former chair of the Commission for Racial Equality.
Ouseley stresses children's vulnerability to 'the influences of
those closest to them'. 'They are born free of prejudice and bias,'
he writes, 'but they soon pick up those in the home...'[13] Later on
in the manual, Lane writes:

> Unless specific and ongoing action is taken with most young
> children to encourage the development of positive attitudes to
> racial differences, it is likely that from the day they are born,
> they are learning the beginnings of racial and often racially
> prejudiced attitudes – just as they are learning the beginnings of
> language.[14]

Scholars of child development might question whether young
children really are mere 'sponges', soaking up and then expressing every influence around them. Historians might take issue
with the idea that people in Britain today – whether black or
white – hold the same ideas about race and racism as they did
in the 1970s. Sociologists might point to the rather disturbing
consequences of advocating that officials use a programme of
'specific and ongoing action' to encourage young children to
develop a particular set of ideas.

But leaving all these important questions aside, it is worth
reflecting on what the self-appointed scourges of early years
racism view as an enlightened approach. For in their view, the
problem lies not in treating black and white children as different, but in treating them the same.

'Adopting a "colour-blind" approach is likely to reinforce
White children's feelings of superiority...' argues Babette

Brown in her 1998 book *Unlearning Discrimination in the Early Years*. 'The claim to "treat children all the same"', she writes, 'is neither likely nor desirable… [It] runs the risk of equating "they are all the same" with "they are all White".'[15]

In a 2009 book aimed at 'policy makers and school managers', Dr Sally Elton-Chalcraft describes her research, revealing how nine- and 10-year-olds internalise the prevailing western mindset — 'and this mindset is racist', proclaims the book's cover, lest we are in any doubt. Elton-Chalcraft had found that many children in her study 'seem to hold anti-racist views', but tended to answer her questions on race with 'we're all the same'. 'This masks their denial of the existence of white privilege', says Elton-Chalcraft: 'Colour-blindness denies a child's identity and may also deny that prejudice exists and may be constantly experienced.'[16]

Lane's NCB volume asserts that 'all children's racial identities — their perceptions of themselves as belonging to a valued group as well as being an individual person — are important', affirming that 'white children's racial identity is important too'.[17] 'Research from Britain, the United States, New Zealand and Australia', writes Lane, 'has provided evidence that children as young as two or three years old notice racial differences.'[18] Citing a 1991 conference report to EYTARN, and a 1985 paper from the *Journal of Negro Education*, Lane states that 'researchers also found that the failure to recognise children's "blackness" damaged some black children's view of themselves and that children's racial identity is crucial for their successful development'.[19]

In these accounts, it appears that children cannot win either way. If they express an awareness of different skin colour, they are reflecting the racist assumptions transmitted to them by an allegedly racist adult population; if they do not remark on difference, they have been inculcated into a 'colour blindness' that is, itself, racist. No wonder, then, that young children can be deemed to reflect racism — because everything they do, when seen through a particular lens, can be labelled as such.

During the time I spent in primary schools on the Essex project, discussed in the Introduction, drama sessions asked children to identify themselves in terms of race. Yet the tutors found themselves under pressure—from the children—to explain why they were promoting pride in skin colour. 'We were told... it's what's on the inside that matters', retorted several children. I recorded a child saying, 'I didn't think the colour of skin had any importance'—'That's very interesting', came the response. After this session, a white boy asks if he should be proud too. On tape he says, 'White people are a group, it's not just white people being racist'. What should anyone make of this response?[20] I came away from the sessions just as confused as the children about what the 'right answer' was supposed to be.

Wounding words

A book by Professor Chris Gaine, published in 2005, aimed at 'supporting everyone in education', cites a 1986 study showing how primary school teachers fail to take children's allegations of racism seriously.[21] According to Gaine, Professor of Applied Social Policy at University College, Chichester, this study revealed 'a three stage denial: it's not happening; all right it's happening but it's not racial; okay it's racial but it's not serious'. '[T]his denial still goes on', says Gaine; arguing further that 'racist name-calling has a unique power: it has more echoes in the real and adult world of discrimination and injustice than any other form of insult traded between children'.

Sidestepping any differences specific to 'the real and adult world of discrimination' of 1986, Gaine's priority is to make a point about twenty-first-century Britain. Here, it seems, nothing much has changed, and any playground name-calling seeming to correspond to 'okay it's racial' must surely correlate directly with the endemic racism in the outside world. For Gaine, it seems, certain words or phrases, once uttered by children, represent airborne acts of racism—regardless of the status or intentions of the speaker.

Government guidance published in 2006, a year after Gaine's book, made the same correlation between the playground and the world at large. *Bullying Around Racism, Religion and Culture* stressed the overarching seriousness of 'racist' playground insults: 'People don't get murdered for being fat or for having ginger hair, or for wearing glasses, or having spots on their faces.'[22]

In the adult world, beyond the primary or nursery school gate, occurrences of racial prejudice and discrimination can certainly be more serious than, for example, the derision faced by overweight people. But is it reasonable to impose a standard rooted in the adult world on to children? At school, children construct their own milieu where being fat or spotty or impaired in some obvious way exists on an equal footing with any other insult-inspiring difference.[23] The fact that people don't get murdered for being fat is of little comfort to school children who are mercilessly targeted for such an attribute.

And indeed, when looking through school incident forms, the handwritten descriptions from teachers often reveal, predictably, the 'perpetrator' claiming to have been provoked: 'you fat XXXX', or 'fatty', appear again and again. When a child feels the sting of such an insult their instinct is to reciprocate with whatever is likely to hurt the most. If the message of the school is 'racist insults are more hurtful', a good sting-back to a black child will come readily to mind (although 'chocolate bar' or 'chocolate face' appears to come more readily to primary school kids than anything else). In this context, the fat child will probably pay a higher price. He or she will be officially reprimanded for having caused a 'racist incident': and back in the playground, the next insult they face may well be, 'you fat racist'.

But the fact that official guidance refuses to see taunts based on skin colour as 'just another' form of playground spat creates a circular problem. Children's insults are imputed, from the start, with the same import as those used by adults, and assumed to have the same effect. This in turn means that the words become invested with a power that goes way beyond what an eight-year-old child might mean when he or she utters the phrase 'chocolate face'. So *Bullying Around Racism, Religion and Culture* states:

> The distinctive feature of a racist attack or insult is that a person is attacked not as an individual, as in most other offences, but as the representative of a family, community or group. Other members of the same group, family or community are in consequence made to feel threatened and intimidated as well. So it is not just the pupil who is attacked who feels unwelcome or marginalised. 'When they call me a Paki,' explains nine-year-old Sereena, 'it's not just me they're hurting. It's all my family and all other black people too.'[24]

Of course, racial insults have a long and dishonourable history. They have been, as Sereena indicates, bound up with wider prejudices against particular communities and ethnic groups, and used as a verbal weapon to underline how unwelcome, or unaccepted, non-white people are. But what gives such words their power is the context in which they are uttered and received. As I argued in previous chapters, the context of Britain today is very different to that of the 1980s, when the term 'Paki' would be uttered and received by people well aware of its wider racist connotations. And, crucially, children are not adults. They experience, and interact with, the world as it is now, rather than as it was 30 years ago.

In the playgrounds of today, children are aware that certain words are 'racist'—in the sense that they know they are very bad things to say. But what they mean when they utter these words is not designed to hurt the recipient's family, let alone 'all other black people'. Despite the alternate reality depicted by anti-racist policies, the playground communities of twenty-first-century Britain are increasingly fizzing with a multi-cultured, multi-ethnic symbiosis that is, by its very nature, an anti-racialising process.[25] In this context, surely before reacting to the words that children use, we should consider what they actually mean by them.

This even goes for the word 'nigger': arguably the most taboo of any insults today. 'It is a loaded word with a weight of history behind it', says the black British comedian Ava Vidal, speculating that it is 'perhaps the last word that Stephen Lawrence heard as he lay bleeding to death'.[26] Vidal is a patron of the schools educational charity Show Racism the Red Card. Fellow comedian, US-born Reginald D. Hunter, uses 'nigga' in his stand-up routine. Furious at Hunter, Vidal adds, 'It is almost certainly the last word that many black men from Hunter's home town of Atlanta, Georgia heard before they were lynched'. Commenting on the uproar after Hunter's perform-ance at the Professional Footballer's Association (PFA) annual awards dinner, Ava Vidal was by no means alone in scolding his use of 'nigga'.[27] The Football Association (FA) charity Kick it Out, chaired by Sir Herman Ouseley, also reprimanded Hunter: '…Kick it Out condemns racial slurs, the use of the n-word irrespective of context…'[28]

For Vidal, the problem with the word 'nigger' is precisely the context that has surrounded its use: it is a 'loaded word'. But its use today is condemned, as Kick it Out puts it, 'irrespective of context'. When the *present-day* context is stripped away from the use of words whose taboo character has been provided by their *historical* context, children stand no chance.

When children today use the n-word as their sting-back rebuke they will only have — at best — a partial knowledge of the adult bigotry which fuels its insulting potential. They will not have access to the full range of knowledge, concepts and emo-tion which lead so many adults to flinch at a word like 'nigger'. They will gradually work out why the majority of adults con-sider 'nigger' to be so offensive that it should never be uttered (except by coded reference to the 'n-word'), and why 'Paki' is almost as bad and why 'white trash' isn't nearly so bad. Until then, anti-racists would do well to remember that children (despite being labelled as 'perpetrators' one day and 'victims' the next) simply do not understand the world in the same way as they do.

In the real world of schools, the playground is a frenetic, messy place colonised by children who will insist on behaving — well, childishly. The 'customs and traditions' of this social group dictate that they fall out, make up, fall out again; they show off, use 'inappropriate' language and are notorious for their flippant cruelty. Official anti-racism disavows the childish sphere, preferring to view it as a maelstrom of abuse and a breeding ground for racism, which must be cleansed by the appropriate interventions.

But explaining to a child that the 'racist' insult they have used attacks their classmate's identity, family, community and traditions does not help them to understand either the history of racism or the world as it is today. At worst, it fractures and racialises children's friendships and causes confusion: 'racism' becomes defined as a forbidden utterance with the power to wound. As children grow older, the sermons on racism given by adults must seem increasingly facile, especially when a Kick it Out 'role model', who was awarded a CBE, is caught using the forbidden n-word.[29] Or when they notice Vidal's stand-up act contains hilarious but, in essence, cruel references to her daughter's weight ('she's fucking massive!'), and that her comedy hero is the n-word touting Chris Rock.[30]

Dutiful schools can, of course, extract 'racist incidents' from their pupils' frenetic break-time life, from disputes in class and even from the language and thoughts expressed in classroom discussions. In east London these may include Bangledeshi children insulting each other with the words 'Kala Bandar' (black monkey). In other areas of London, banter between black pupils greeting one another with 'wos'up nigga!' is duly recorded as a racist incident. Words used by African Caribbean pupils to describe African pupils get recorded. Now that homo-phobic incidents are starting to be recorded it's interesting to note how African Caribbean pupils' use of 'batty boy' often requires teachers to reach for homophobic *and* racist incident forms in instances where, for example, the victim has turned perpetrator by replying, 'fuck off, broccoli head'.[31]

The tip of the iceberg (again)

The nature of specific 'racist incidents', as described by teachers on reporting forms, has never been of much interest to official anti-racists. From its inception, the purpose of incident reporting was to enable the government to ostentatiously demonstrate its compliance with legislation. For the more zealous town hall official, aggregated figures for racist incidents in schools only meant one thing—the racism of white society slowly unveiled.

In 2005, Essex council's response to its yearly totals for primary and secondary schools (a figure of 1,566 racist incidents) was to view it as a stage in the unveiling process. Schools were not reporting enough. Among 'actions to be taken', officials listed training sessions for teachers and letters to schools pointing out that 'high levels of reported incidents are the result of good practice rather than the converse'.[32] Schools must instil an ethos that actively seeks to 'identify and eradicate all manifestations of racism, however trivial they may seem'. The implicit instruction to schools was, therefore, to throw out a dragnet into the playground and haul in as many incidents as possible—or rather, to maintain 'a climate in which all members of the school community are given permission to raise concerns about anything that might be perceived as racist, including insensitive use of language, comments, jokes, mimicry etc.'.[33]

Equalities officials know full well that a typical school incident is likely to be a spat involving phrases like 'you're a milky bar'/'well then you're a mars bar'. But when aggregated incident figures fall into the hands of the news media, the role of official experts in aggrandising the spectre of serious and endemic and frequently violent schoolyard racism is striking. In 2007, when *Channel 4 News* reported that 95,000 incidents had been gathered from 90 authorities across four years, it reported the statistic together with a case of an Asian child being persistently bullied by white children. As always, an expert was on hand. 'These statistics are just the tip of the iceberg', said Professor Heidi Safia Mirza of the Institute of Education. 'There are a lot of young people who don't want to report this because they are too embarrassed or frightened to do so.'[34]

The myth generated from incident reporting remains persistent. In 2012 it surfaced again, following a BBC freedom of information survey of 90 local authorities.[35] A spokesperson from the campaign group Show Racism the Red Card claimed that the 87,000 incidents recorded over four years from a sample of local authorities 'are just the tip of the iceberg'.[36] On a Birmingham radio talk-show, another anti-racism official frothed at my counterclaim that most of these incidents involve the trivial insults and banter of primary-aged kids. 'Oh my God, what a sad day this is,' boomed Maxie Hayles, 'what a sad day to hear someone talking about "trivial incidents" by children, childish behaviour.' Hayles continued:

> The reality is that the very fabric of this society is racist and institutional racism is rife here. The local authority and schools need to take over the playground... Some of those young people should be prosecuted. The parents should be held responsible and educated because we're breeding a lot of young racist thugs. In a few years we won't be different from any other countries in Europe.

The presenter, Adrian Goldberg, interjected at this point: 'I've got to say my experience of schools isn't that at all Maxie, that's a little harsh, we're talking about a minority here!' Hayles was irritated: 'A minority! Are you kidding me? You just told me that we've got a situation where 80,000 incidents have been recorded in schools over a four-year period!'[37]

'Look, no hands!' — Did the Coalition Government abandon racist incident reporting?

After the Conservative-Liberal Democrat Coalition government came to power in 2010, it published a provisional ten-page schools guidance document titled 'Preventing and Tackling Bullying: advice for headteachers, staff and governing bodies'.[38] This replaced a voluminous 'suite' of official guidance called 'Safe to Learn'. The new government was keen to demonstrate its hands off approach by appearing to cut red tape and hand autonomy back to school leaders. Despite an emphasis on the need for schools to attend to a range of prejudice-related bullying, the new guidance made clear that schools must exercise their own judgment and devise their own policies. This applied to the recording of all bullying incidents — schools could choose to do it or not.[39]

Many took this as an abandonment of the legal duty to record and report 'racist incidents'. In fact, there had never been a legal duty (although local authorities had tended to promote this view). After amended race legislation came on-stream in 2002, compliance with statutory *general duties* around race issues became widely interpreted as necessarily involving racist incident reporting, as per the Macpherson Report's recommendation #15.[40] In other words, many education authorities promoted incident reporting as a 'requirement' that schools were expected to fulfil in order to demonstrate they were taking race issues seriously (and thus allowing the authority to demonstrate its compliance with legislation).

The apparent abandonment, by the Coalition Government, of the 'racist incident' requirement (legal or otherwise) was reinforced by its guidance speaking only of 'bullying'. The new advice had, indeed, sidestepped a key feature of racist incident reporting, enshrined in the Macpherson definition, which was that an 'incident' did not have to be 'bullying': it need only be *an incident perceived to be racist by the victim or any other person.*[41]

But regardless of the new government's 'hands-off' rhetoric, the prospect of new equalities legislation and forthcoming Ofsted requirements had already ensured that most Local Education Authorities (LEAs) took a cautious 'business as usual' approach.

In September 2011 the Manifesto Club published a second report, titled *Leave Those Kids Alone*. Its central finding was that schools' racist incident figures for 2009/10 were running at a similar pitch to previous years, but were now joined by data on other 'hate' categories such as 'homophobic incidents'. A tally of 152 local authorities in England and Wales showed that, in the previous year (2008/09), 30,000 racist incidents were reported by schools. Once again, most incidents came from primary schools and the vast majority were verbal.[42]

Ahead of the publication of *Leave Those Kids Alone*, a sneak preview of our 2008/09 figures led to front page headlines in the *Daily Mail*.[43] By this time even the Runnymede Trust was acknowledging, albeit begrudgingly, some of the issues raised by *The Myth of Racist Kids,* such as the 'time consuming practice of recording often very small incidents'.[44] It also acknowledged past criticism coming from schools, which had cited 'inherent bureaucracy' and teachers' confusion 'about what such incidents entail'.[45]

Today, ascertaining up-to-date figures is hard. The scale of recording has become obscured by the fact that a steady flow of LEAs have, for now at least, concluded that the Coalition guidance releases them from any obligation to collect the data: this task is now regarded as the responsibility of individual schools. A spot check that I conducted of 31 LEAs in January 2014 revealed that around half (14) were continuing to collect data, and 13 out of 31 LEAs told me of 4,348 racist incidents for year 2012/13.

If we were to assume that the schools covered by these 13 authorities are representative of all schools in England and Wales, then it is safe to assume that schools are recording racist incidents at similar levels to the past. In other words: the practice of schools recording 'racist incidents' continues unabated and at a level we can estimate as 30,000 a year.

Figures that I collected under the Freedom of Information Act about primary schools in Birmingham, where the council has ceased to collect data, suggests that at playground level the policy remains proactive. Moreover, schools continue to collect racist *incidents* as well as racist *bullying.* This is not surprising, given that most schools take requirements by the schools inspection body Ofsted very much to heart.

The Ofsted School Inspection handbook, published in September 2012, makes it clear that inspectors will request logs of *racist* incidents and incidents of bullying, including homophobic bullying. A briefing paper for Ofsted inspectors stated they must check that schools have 'clear procedures for dealing with prejudice-related bullying and incidents, and appropriate staff training that equips staff to identify and deal with this effectively'.[46]

The Equalities Act, which came into force in April 2011, intended to simplify existing anti-discrimination law by placing it under one umbrella of legislation. Section 149 of the Equalities Act entails a *general duty* requiring public bodies to have 'due regard' for 'fostering good relations', eliminating discrimination (including harassment and victimisation) and advancing equality of opportunity. The Act included a new 'Public Sector Equality Duty' (PSED) incorporating *specific duties* on race, disability and gender but added additional 'protected categories' — age, religion or belief, sexual orientation, pregnancy and maternity and gender reassignment. To demonstrate 'due regard' for its general duties schools must show they have carried out their specific duties in relation to the protected categories. The publication of anti-bullying policies, equalities targets, curriculum and staff training materials and pupil surveys all count as evidence of compliance.

Schools seeking to gain or maintain 'outstanding' Ofsted ratings have quickly learnt that demonstrating compliance with equalities duties means inspections can be faced with confidence. And, given Ofsted's predilection for evaluating the behaviour and especially the 'safeguarding' of pupils, one straightforward and demonstrable action schools will adopt is the keeping of prejudice-related bullying and incidents records. It is likely that many of those LEAs that have stopped collecting data from schools will soon resume as they come to realise that they, too, need to demonstrate 'due regard' to equalities duties in relation to state-maintained schools; and that an LEA's decision to stop collecting and monitoring schools data will become regarded as a failure to show 'due regard'.

Welcome to inter-victimisation!

When Education Secretary Michael Gove recently promised a Stonewall conference a 'clampdown on the use of homophobic language in the school playground', he was not proposing the Equalities Act be amended to elevate anti-gay hate above other protected 'hate' categories.[47] We can expect similar statements to be used in relation to cyberbullying; sexist, transphobic or sexualised bullying and incidents; and incidents involving disabled children or those with special educational needs (SEN). In the meantime, schools will continue to record racist incidents, and expand their recording regime into the various other target categories. Moreover, in the latest draft of government guidance on bullying, schools are recommended to utilise the workshops and education packs of just three organisations: Show Racism the Red Card, Kick it Out and the Anne Frank Trust.[48]

A sweep through the incident forms sent to me by Brighton and Birmingham primary schools show racist and homophobic incidents reported routinely — with Brighton schools gradually beginning to include 'prejudiced-based' incidents relating to gender identity and sexism, disability and SEN, and even categories not stipulated by legislation such as 'home circumstances' — as in the insult, 'your mum lives in a bin'.

We can only pity the teacher who will have to decipher and document a proliferating set of prejudice-related incidents arising from a single playground dispute. How, for example, will they untangle competing claims that A called B's trainers 'gay' or that B, in fact, first called A, who is disabled, 'lame', leading to A's friend C calling B 'battyman' and B's friend D calling C, who is African Caribbean, 'blacky'?

In Birmingham, primary school incidents marked as 'racist' seem absurd enough by themselves: 'A's mother reported that A had said at the weekend that a group of boys in his class had been saying that they shouldn't have anything to do with white people. She said A had been upset by this. B said he was not allowed to go to Christian houses because it's part of his religion. He doesn't think he should play with white people. He said no-one is telling him this, he just knows it because he's a Muslim.'[49] Another incident concerned a football match: '[Asian child A] called [Asian child B] "Kala" (black) after he was pushed away from goals by him.' Yet another describes how, 'following a disagreement A stated "I'd better not touch her in case I turn black"', noting the perpetrator as 'Pakistan heritage' and the victim as 'Black Caribbean'.

Among the most absurd from Birmingham were, 'Year 3 boy called a white boy a Paki and a black boy a Paki', 'Child A called child B an African Rat, and C a rat. Child A said "I know I shouldn't have called it her because I'm black as well"', and 'Year 2 boy called a boy on his table at lunchtime "Chocolate Face"'. In almost every case, the forms list, under 'actions', 'letters home' and numerous other actions. In the example above ('Chocolate Face'), actions included the child perpetrator sent to the head, to 'the pastoral team', and notes, 'class teacher and TA [teaching assistant] spoke to him as well. TA spoke to step-dad and mum'.

Brighton's most absurd examples included: 'Though there was no direct recipient, Child A was pulling his eyes sideways with his fingers saying "I'm Chinese" on his way to lunch', and 'Child B was agitated by Child C on his table. His response was to declare to his table that he thinks all white people are mean and he doesn't like them'. A Brighton school also lists an incident from its nursery-wing for children aged three and four: 'child looking at pictures of people with different eye colours and said "yuk not black" and discarded all the black faces, then said I want a boy. Action: sent to counsellor.'

By including more 'prejudice-related' categories, Brighton's primary school incidents do at least offer a less racialised picture of childish conflict: but this picture is arguably even worse, in that it takes every slight and insult with grave seriousness. Flippant 'you are gay/that is so gay' incidents occur in abundance; 'you're a girl' (presumably said to a boy) is recorded as 'sexism/sexual', 'you're a spaz and a lesbian' is recorded as 'other' (perhaps to save reaching for two separate forms) and 'fat bucket of KFC' is recorded under the category of 'prejudice relating to appearance'.

Viewed together, the Birmingham and Brighton incident forms *should* offer anti-racists a reasonably positive race-equality message — in the sense that children of *any* ethnicity can be nasty little sods. Of course, if there were such a thing as 'harmonious incident reporting', there would be infinitely more forms to fill out showing the same children doggedly engaged in acts of kindness, forging common bonds and making friends. But, argue anti-racist campaigners, this misses the point. Jenny Bourne, of the Institute of Race Relations (IRR), attacks my naive view of children, in which (she says) 'human nature, untrammelled, finds a natural *modus vivendi* with the "other"'.[50]

In the IRR's riposte to my report—an article, from November 2009, titled 'The Myth of Anti-Racist Kids'—Bourne accepts that 'monitoring a problem via form-filling is always going to be a somewhat blunt instrument'. For Bourne, though, there is no alternative to such bureaucratic attempts to train teachers to monitor every potentially racist incident among children. And, as she makes clear in the final paragraph of her article, even proposing an alternative is itself an apology for racism:

> At a time when the BNP is targeting children for its youth wing and yet teacher training still does not contain a compulsory element on race and diversity, the Manifesto Club's position on children and racism cannot be dismissed as some esoteric, polemical posing about childhood innocence *à la* Jean-Jacques Rousseau. It is downright dangerous, especially at a time when the rightwing press just cannot wait to champion such half-baked views.[51]

We're all children now...

The conviction with which anti-racist campaigners presume no alternative to officially-imposed measures to identify, monitor and 'clamp down' on children's apparently racist taunts has some serious consequences for children and adults alike. Children's everyday games, interactions and fallings-out are elevated and problematised to a level far beyond playground banter.

Children are perceived as mini-adults, investing words with a prejudice and power that bears no relation either to their age or the context in which they are living and playing. Meanwhile adults, as we discussed in previous chapters, are treated like children, who must accept the increasing regulation of their words and interactions through policies designed to enforce diversity and stamp out any expression that could be deemed, by official arbiters, to be racist.

But as Bourne's riposte to my own work indicates, the biggest casualty in this process is the capacity to debate. Even questioning the orthodoxy that children are both repositories and agents of a poisonous racist sensibility is seen as a heresy, a 'dangerous' apology for the things that must not be said. As I argue in the next chapter, the result of all this is not the enlightened, tolerant society that anti-racist campaigners claim to be constructing. It can best be described, rather, as an enormous mess, out of which nobody benefits – not even those who make the rules.

Endnotes:

1   NASUWT (2009) 'Manifesto Group Report Unacceptable and Irresponsible Say NASUWT', 29 October. Accessed 20 May 2014. Available at: http://centrallobby.politicshome.com/stakeholder-websites/press-releases/press-release-details/newsarticle/manifesto-group-report-unacceptable-and-irresponsible-says-nasuwt///sites/nasuwt/

2   Beckford, M. (2009) 'Schools Report 40,000 Cases of Racism a Year', *Daily Telegraph*, 29 October. Accessed 16 May 2014. Available at: http://www.telegraph.co.uk/education/educationnews/6454857/Schools-report-40000-cases-of-racism-a-year.html

3   Hart, A. (2009) *The Myth of Racist Kids: Anti-Racist Policy and the Regulation of School Life,* London: The Manifesto Club. Examples of incident forms are included at the start of the report. Accessed 09 June 2014. Available at: http://www.manifestoclub.com/mythracistkids

4   Department for Education and Skills (2006) *Bullying Around Racism, Religion and Culture,* London: HMSO, p48.

5   Hart, A. (2009) *Op. cit.*, p64.

6   *Ibid.*, p15.

7   EYTARN are listed as having made a written submission in Appendix 17 of the Macpherson Report. On the subject of the 'learnt behaviour' of racist children the report quotes schools research undertaken by Cardiff Race Equality Counsel cited by witness Chief Constable Burden. Burden told the inquiry that this research had revealed 50 percent of racist incidents involved children under 16 – and 25 percent of those had involved children between 6 and 10. See: Macpherson, W. (1999) *The Stephen Lawrence Inquiry,* UK Government Command Paper 4262–1, Ch 2.19.

8   Brown, B. (2001) *Combating Discrimination: Persona Dolls in Action,*
     Stoke-on-Trent: Trentham Books, p39. Brown is making a reference
     to Macpherson (Ch 2.19) who is, himself, referring to the testimony
     of Chief Constable Burden; *Ibid.*

9   *Ibid.*

10   Chambers, C., Funge, S., Harris, G., and Williams, C. (1997)
     Celebrating Identity: A Resource Manual, Stoke-on-Trent: Trentham
     Books, p15. Studies conducted in 1947 by Kenneth and Mamie Clark
     seemed to establish that a racist society will damage a child's
     'identity development'.

11   Hraba, J., and Grant, G. (1970) 'Black is Beautiful: A Re-examination
     of Racial Preference and Identification'. See: Gary Sturt: http://
     www.garysturt.free-online.co.uk/hraba.htm. Accessed 20 May 2014.

12   Lane, J. (2008) *Young Children and Racial Justice: Taking action for racial
     equality in the early years – understanding the past, thinking about the
     present, planning for the future,* London: National Children's Bureau
     (NCB), pxii.

13   *Ibid.,* pix–x.

14   *Ibid.,* p88.

15   Brown, B. (1998) *Unlearning Discrimination in the Early Years,* Stoke-
     on-Trent: Trentham Books, p54.

16   Elton-Chalcraft, S. (2009) *'It's Not Just About Black and White, Miss':
     Children's Awareness of Race,* Stoke- on-Trent: Trentham Books,
     pp132–4.

17   Lane, J. (2008) *Young Children and Racial Justice: Taking action for racial
     equality in the early years – understanding the past, thinking about the
     present, planning for the future,* London: National Children's Bureau
     (NCB), p135.

18   *Ibid.,* p88.

19   *Ibid.* Lane's sources are listed as Gay, G. (1985) 'Implications of
     Selected Models of Ethnic Identity Development for Educators',
     Journal of Negro Education, 54(1); and Maxime, J. (1991) *Towards a
     Transcultural Approach to Working with Under-Sevens,* conference
     report for the Early Years Trainers Anti-Racist Network (EYTARN)
     and the National Children's Bureau.

20   Hart, A. (2009) *Op. cit.,* p26.

21   Gaine, C. (2005) *We're All White, Thanks: The Persisting Myth About
     'White' Schools,* Stoke-on-Tent: Trentham Books, p108. Gaine cites a
     1986 study by S. Akhtar and I. Stronach titled '"They Call Me
     Blacky" – A Story of Everyday Racism in Primary Schools', *Times
     Educational Supplement,* 19 September, p23.

22   Department for Education and Skills (2006) *Bullying Around Racism,
     Religion and Culture,* London: HMSO, p50. The same wording
     appears in 2011 guidance issued by the Welsh government: see
     http://learning.wales.gov.uk/docs/learningwales/publications/12

1128abraceen.pdf

23   Professor Gaine seems to agree: 'I am not claiming that racism is worse than other verbal abuse or that it must always take priority… Many young people's lives are made a misery by the name-calling they suffer for all kinds of real or imagined attributes…', but then seems to disagree; '…But there is something different and special about racist abuse…' See: Gaine, C. (2005) *Op. cit.*, p111 and 112.

24   Department for Education and Skills (2006) *Bullying Around Racism, Religion and Culture, Op. cit.*, p52. The advice also appeared on the government website TeacherNet and can be viewed here: http://webarchive.nationalarchives.gov.uk/20040722012353/http://teachernet.gov.uk/wholeschool/behaviour/tacklingbullying/racist bullying/responding/. Accessed 22 May 2014. The majority of young people's quotes selected for use in government advice appear to come from DfES-organised 'focus group meetings, individual meetings, two conferences and a series of workshops with young people aged from 5 to 18': Richardson, R., and Miles, B. (2008) *Racist Incidents and Bullying in Schools*, Stoke-on-Trent: Trentham Books, p9.

25   The idea that an ethnically diverse and harmonious playground of children is, in itself, evidence of their colour-blindness is sometimes dismissed as the 'contact hypothesis' (to presume that the existence of inter-ethnic friendship groups must somehow imply an absence of racial prejudice). See: Troyna, B., and Hatcher, R. (1992) *Racism in Children's Lives*, London: Routledge, p25.

26   Vidal, A. (2013) 'Why was Reginald D Hunter Ever Booked for the PFA Awards?', *Guardian*, 30 April. Accessed 17 May 2014. Available at: http://www.theguardian.com/commentisfree/2013/apr/30/reginald-d-hunter-pfa-awards

27   See: Riach, J. (2013) 'Reginald D Hunter's Comedy Set at PFA Awards was "Huge Mistake"', *Guardian*, 29 April. Accessed 17 May 2014. Available at: http://www.theguardian.com/football/2013/apr/29/clarke-carlisle-reginald-hunter-pfa-awards

28   *Ibid.*

29   When former Kick it Out trustee and ex-Chelsea defender Paul Elliot used 'nigger' in an angry, *private* text message he was obliged to resign from his various Football Association roles. Somehow his text message was leaked to the press. It didn't matter that this was a private spat between two black former players, the rules of 'zero tolerance' anti-racism, vociferously campaigned for by Elliot himself, had to be applied. See also: Drayton, J. (2013) 'Anti-Racism Campaigner Elliot Resigns from FA After His N-Word Rant at Rufus', *Daily Mail*, 23 February. Accessed 20 May 2014. Available at: http://www.dailymail.co.uk/sport/football/article-2283318/Paul-Elliott-resigns-FA-racism-row-Richard-Rufus.html

30   'Niggas v. Black People' is perhaps Chris Rock's most famous

routine. See: http://www.youtube.com/channel/UCqefeyQtxe2C2
texM8pVW6w

31 Hart, A. (2011) *Leave Those Kids Alone: How Official Hate Speech Regulation Interferes in School Life,* London: The Manifesto Club, p17.

32 See: Essex County Council (2006) 'Scrutiny Panel of the Children, Young People and Schools Policy Development Group CHSC/09/06', 5 April, pp21–3. Accessed on 09 June 2014. Available at: http://tinyurl.com/pcy62d7

33 *Ibid.,* p21.

34 See: *Channel 4 News* (2007) 'Racism in Schools', 24 May. Accessed 05 June 2014. Available at: http://www.channel4.com/news/articles/society/education/revealed+racism+in+schools/529297.html

35 Talwar, D. (2012) 'More than 87,000 Racist Incidents Recorded in Schools', *BBC News*, 23 May. Accessed 17 May 2014. Available at: http://www.bbc.co.uk/news/education-18155255

36 Sarah Soyei, of the anti-racism charity Show Racism the Red Card, said 'Unfortunately, the numbers of recorded racist incidents are just the tip of the iceberg'.

37 BBC Radio West Midlands (2012) *The Adrian Goldberg Show*, 10 March.

38 See: Department for Education (2014) *Preventing and Tackling Bullying*, London: HMSO, March. Accessed 20 May 2014. Available at: https://www.gov.uk/government/uploads/system/uploads/attachment_data/file/288444/preventing_and_tackling_bullying_march14.pdf

39 *Ibid.,* p9.

40 Following the Macpherson Inquiry, the Race Relations (Amendment) Act 2000 placed public bodies under a legal duty to: 'Have due regard to the need to eliminate unlawful discrimination and to promote equality of opportunity and good relations between persons of different racial groups.' See: http://www.legislation.gov.uk/ukpga/2000/34/notes/division/3

41 It is, nonetheless, the case that the government (as of 2014) defers to certain anti-racist charities who make the Macpherson distinction on incidents (as opposed to bullying) clear. In the latest draft of Coalition guidance (March 2014), under 'Further Information' and 'Racism', the guidance lists three links: Show Racism the Red Card, Kick it Out and the Anne Frank Trust (Department for Education (2014) *Op. cit.*, p11).

42 Hart, A. (2011) *Op. cit.*

43 Harris. S. (2011) '30,000 Pupils Branded as Bigots…', *Daily Mail*, 17 January. Accessed 17 May 2014. Available at: http://www.dailymail.co.uk/news/article-1348089/30-000-pupils-branded-racist-homophobic-bigots-teachers-nursery.html

44 See: Runnymede Trust (2010) 'Runnymede Trust Written Consulta-

tion Response to "Recording and Reporting Incidents of Bullying
Between Pupils, and Incidents of Abuse against School Staff"'.
Accessed 20 May 2014. Available at: http://www.runnymedetrust.
org/uploads/policyResponses/BullyingIncidentsResponse.pdf.
Runnymede's Senior Research & Policy Analyst Dr Debbie Weekes-
Bernard says, 'There are many schools that have duly recorded and
reported incidents and though there has been some degree of con-
sternation at the numbers of incidents reported, which is linked to a
worrying wider set of issues about those who promote race equality
in schools and concern about the divisions and unnecessary awareness about difference that this can cause, awareness about these
incidents is necessary and important'.

45   *Ibid.*
46   See: Ofsted (2011) 'Briefings and Information for Use During
     Inspections of Maintained Schools and Academies' (Inspecting
     Equalities p11). Accessed on 18 May 2014. Available at: http://
     www.ofsted.gov.uk/resources/briefings-and-information-for-use-
     during-inspections-of-maintained-schools-and-academies-january-
     201, and for comment on Ofsted's requirement see: http://www.
     insted.co.uk/recording-reporting-2011.pdf (p5).
47   Garner, R. (2013) 'Michael Gove Pledges Clampdown on Use of
     Homophobic Language in Schools Playgrounds', *Independent*, 5 July.
     Accessed 17 May 2014. Available at: http://www.independent.co.
     uk/news/education/education-news/michael-gove-pledges-
     clampdown-on-use-of-homophobic-language-in-school-
     playgrounds-8691132.html
48   See: Department for Education (2014) *Op. cit.*, p11.
49   In most cases the forms sent to me by schools have names of
     children blotted out by marker pen. I have added 'Child A' or 'A'
     etc. in place of the redacted names.
50   Bourne, J. (2009) 'The Myth of Anti-Racist Kids', *Institute of Race
     Relations*, 5 November. Accessed 17 May. Available at: http://www.
     irr.org.uk/news/the-myth-of-anti-racist-kids/
51   *Ibid.*

Chapter Five

The Mess it Makes

Case 1: The defamation of Varndean School

I am often challenged to explain why I insist the spectre of racism in UK schools is a 'myth'. After one university debating event, I was asked to explain why, if this is indeed the case, 'research has shown there are more than 30,000 racist incidents reported by schools every year'. I pointed out that it was actually my own research, for the Manifesto Club, that had shown this—and my point was that to regard it as evidence of 'racism' is a mistake, for the reasons detailed in the previous chapter.

But my challenger immediately responded: 'So what about that secondary school in Brighton? You live in Brighton! It's the school where black children are regularly attacked and racially abused by gangs of white children.' He had been alerted to this story by the Institute of Race Relation's (IRR) monthly newsletter, and by the European 'Hate Crime' news archive, produced by I-CARE, the Internet Centre for Anti-Racism Europe.[1] 'Didn't you hear about it?', he demanded.

Ah, Varndean School—this is one of two secondary schools that my son might go to. I had heard about the 'racism' saga from numerous parents in my neighbourhood who have kids at the school. But they hadn't heard the story from their children: they had read about it in the local newspaper. 'BRIGHTON SCHOOLGIRL HOUNDED BY RACIST BULLIES', ran the headline.[2] A few days later the story resurfaced, this time as 'RACISM PROBE AT VARNDEAN SCHOOL'.[3] The hounding of one girl had now broadened to multiple cases, revealing 'a culture of racial abuse'. These press reports had then passed from the *Argus* to the IRR bulletin and I-CARE, propagating across the web and available to anyone searching 'racist + bullying + schools'.[4]

In the first press report we learn that 'a gang of racist yobs has waged a four-month hate campaign against a teenage girl. The 14-year-old girl, who is mixed race, has been called appalling names, taunted on the internet and even threatened with a knuckleduster. The mother of the Varndean School student from Brighton, said the bigoted abuse had "seriously damaged" her daughter'. In the second, we learn that, in a school brochure, a picture of the girl had been defaced with racist graffiti. The child responsible had been excluded.

Abigail Sinclair, a community worker from the anti-racism charity Mosaic, told the *Argus* reporter that she was 'in contact with the parents of six children at the school who had complained of repeated verbal and physical racial abuse'. Apparently the 'majority' of school racism cases dealt with by the charity over the past 18 months had involved students at Varndean. 'Many children do not feel safe and secure in that school', said Sinclair. 'The problem is getting worse and I am fearful for the future.' Both the *Argus* reports include responses from the school leadership and the council. The school 'robustly and vigorously denies any suggestions that there is a culture of such behaviour at Varndean', pointing out that it could not comment in more detail as it had a duty of confidentiality. The council said: 'Work has begun to explore what the issues are and to build on good practice.'

When reading press reports about your own neighbourhood and its local secondary school, opportunities to match the story to the world around you, to what you know or can easily find out, are far greater. To experience media stories about racist bullying in a school in a faraway town is very different. For many of us, a story like this one seems both shocking and plausible—a parent of a child has come forward with allegations, a community worker has backed up and added to the allegations, and the school and the local authority say very little.

We are tempted to conclude it might well be true; that there is surely no smoke without fire.

For avid readers of IRR news bulletins, the Varndean story confirms what they think they already know about racism in society. Should the subject of everyday racism in schools/on council estates/on the streets ever come up, '*that* school in Brighton' is the kind of thing they might now mention, along-side '*that* Panorama expose of Bristol's Southmead estate'[5] or any number of stories about the behaviour of football fans or the latest stop and search figures.

But what actually happened at Varndean School? As is often the case when we look beneath the headlines, the reality is far less clear cut than the recycled stories suggest.

So I'm chatting with a Varndean student who is in the same year group as the mixed-race girl at the centre of the *Argus* story. We'll call this student 'Q'. It is April 2013, some 10 months after the news articles appeared. 'The first I knew was when the story appeared in the paper', Q tells me. 'The problem is that this particular girl is feisty, she rarely stays in the classroom for the whole lesson. She gets sent out because she always has an argument with the teacher.' Q doesn't think this is about racism: 'I couldn't imagine a whole gang of children in the school being racist to one girl — there has to be some other significance here?'

As I chat to Q the possibility of a different explanation emerges — namely the rivalries, the passions, the intense friend-ships of a group of teenage girls, broken then repaired. 'In our year the girls seem to be divided into two groups', says Q. 'The girl in the *Argus* story is a strong personality, she's got a wide circle of friends. I think she had a terrible falling out with a friend. It happened outside of school.'

Almost all of the alleged bullying of this girl, described in the *Argus*, took place *outside of school*. The newspaper states: 'at a funfair in late May, she was set upon by a 20-strong gang of girls and boys. They pushed her around, taunted her and tried to hold her still. To her horror, she saw another girl putting on a knuckleduster and preparing to hit her.' It seems the girl managed to escape the 20-strong gang and run away. In another incident, the girl was reportedly approached in the local park by members of the gang who 'threw bricks at her head'.

It is not surprising that readers of the *Argus* reacted strongly to news of these incidents. Nobody would want their child to be in such a terrifying situation. But the questions that need to be asked are, first, were these *racist* incidents? And second, should a school be held responsible for incidents between children that happen at a funfair, or in the park?

According to Q, the driver for these incidents was not racism, but smouldering rivalries between 14-year-old girls. 'The thing is,' says Q, 'children — when they fall out — say whatever they think will hurt.'

Varndean School's racist incident and bullying log from the year leading up to the *Argus* articles, available via a Freedom of Information request, suggests a school vigilantly recording everything and anything that comes to its attention. Many of the 71 incidents for the year 2011/12 simply state 'racist comment to another student', 'alleged racist comment' or 'name-calling perceived to be racist'. Others state 'racist language in class' or 'racist language in conversation'. Others still describe the incident in a little more detail, ranging from the n-word, Hitler salutes, describing a school cleaner as 'foreign and dangerous', suggesting that '9/11 was justified because the US are attacking Muslims', drawing a swastika and using 'a mock Spanish accent' in front of a Spanish teacher. Q gives the example of a black boy in her year group who has a mixed-race friend: 'they always call each other "nigga" — they think it's funny.'

The policy-driven phenomenon of filtering the everyday rough and tumble of school life for 'racism', which reduces flippant banter, insult-exchange, passionate rivalries and fallings-out to '71 racist incidents', all too easily inspires anti-racists to presume *a culture of racism*. Maybe there was more to it than the statistics: Mosaic had been quoted as being 'in contact' with the parents of six victims of serious (including physical) racist abuse.[6] But when I tried to find out more from Mosaic, the charity refused to talk to me.[7]

The council did talk to me. Councillor Sue Shanks, chair of the Children and Young People Committee, said that the local authority 'does not have an official role investigating stories printed by the *Argus*'; but revealed that the council 'were told by Mosaic that the statement printed in the *Argus* was not one made through official Mosaic channels'.[8] In my Freedom of Information request asking for more information on Mosaic, the council revealed that it had 'no records of the cases referred to in the *Argus*'.[9]

Moreover, the Council's 'racism probe' referred to in the second *Argus* article was, they say, merely a routine monitoring visit of the 'Healthy Schools Team', and not in response to press allegations. The monitoring visit identified 'good practice' and a reduction in 'anonymously reported' bullying, though it also found that 'some students reported that prejudiced language is used by some of their peers'. In other words: the monitoring visit found Varndean to be a pretty normal school.

The fact that Q, whose own circle of close friends includes non-white students, could be so surprised and bemused by the *Argus* reports (and especially the reference to 'a culture of racist abuse') was an early indicator that the 'culture of racism' claim was erroneous. The suggestion that Mosaic had distanced itself from the claims made by its community worker, Abigail Sinclair, was another. A newspaper's sinister depiction of an English school beset by a violent culture of racism began to look suspicious in a different way.

Three factors had brought the story to life. First, a mother's understandably partisan view of her child's account of bullying becomes framed by pre-existing notions that the problem of 'racism' lies at its root (after all, *racist* insults have been uttered). Second, the involvement of anti-racism organisations, such as Mosaic, inflates the idea that this is no one-off incident but rather the tip of the iceberg—an unveiling of a school where serious, including violent, racist incidents are rife. Third, the *Argus* reporting sits permanently online, an ongoing reminder of 'another story' of racism exposed.

Stage by stage the anti-racist narrative is affirmed, evidenced most powerfully by: the mother's view that racism had 'seriously damaged' her daughter; and also by the Mosaic worker for whom a 'culture' of racism runs unchecked. For its part, the council finds itself apparently unable to control the consequences of its own policies, or the actions of partner-organisations like Mosaic.

An anti-racism charity such as Mosaic is likely to work according to Macpherson's definition of 'unwitting', institutional racism. Indeed, according to this definition, my scepticism over the Varndean story and Q's bemusement are themselves symptomatic of a culture of denial — of racism hidden or ignored, unreported, or explained away.

The Macpherson approach recommends that every allegation however small or far-fetched must be taken seriously and investigated. Ironically, in the Varndean case, the council's eagerness to assert the robustness of its monitoring policies and those of the school appeared to trump adherence to its own policy definition of a 'hate' incident. According to the council's own guidelines, a hate incident is any incident 'perceived by the victim or any other person to be motivated by hostility, prejudice or ignorance, based on a person's perceived or actual ethnicity, gender, disability... [etc.]'.[10] And yet, multiple incidents perceived as racist by the Mosaic worker and reported in the local paper were not — it seemed — the council's concern, as these allegations had not come through the correct channels.

In stressing the successful application of its own monitoring procedures, the council came, I suspect, uncomfortably close to inferring that the allegations were indeed erroneous. But to say any more than this — to explicitly and publicly support its school — might expose the council to allegations of ignoring racism. In the officially-mandated fight against 'institutional racism', ignoring allegations of racism simply because they came through the wrong channels, or did not appear on your organisation's monitoring systems, are seen to represent a sure sign of the disease.

In this way, the Varndean affair illustrates not only the tyranny of anti-racism, but also its cowardice. With the local authority caught within this web of contradictory expectation and regulation, the net result was that a vibrant, modern school, with black and minority ethnic students forming around 20 percent[11] of the student body, had been denigrated and hung out to dry, online, forever. Equally pernicious is how the story of Varndean provides the anti-racist narrative with yet another example of 'the problem' that policies are setting out to tackle: policies that result in school interventions that further racialise tensions, and have other destructive effects.

Case 2: The never-ending scandal of golliwogs

'Let's be clear about this', says Lee Jasper. 'A Golliwog is a disgusting White stereotype of an enslaved African that seeks to negate the greatest crime in human history and transform the misery of enslaved Africans into a cartoon figure of fun.'[12]

Many today would assume that this is, indeed, the true story of the golliwog. In fact, its origins are far from clear. Who can really know what malevolent, racist intention (if any) was in the mind of illustrator Florence Kate Upton when, in 1895, she invented the character of the golliwog for a British children's book.[13] In the story, the golliwog appears as 'a horrid sight, the blackest gnome', but quickly becomes lovable with 'a kind face'. Upton, who grew up in New York, was influenced by the US tradition of blackface minstrelsy.[14] The golliwog character was inspired, she wrote later, by a minstrel rag doll she played with as a child.[15]

Some argue the nineteenth-century minstrel theatre ridiculed black people as clown-like and foolish. Others point out that the minstrels, who began as white Americans with blacked-up faces, were later taken over by black performers whose talent and popularity challenged social norms and often irritated whites in the racist south. Either way, Upton had blackface minstrelsy in mind, but with a more innocent intention than Jasper imagines; her golliwog invention was, in a sense, a caricature of a caricature.[16]

The 'wog' part of Upton's 'golliwog' is itself controversial. Was 'Wily Oriental Gentleman' (WOG) a racist term in 1895 — or did 'wog' only emerge as such in the Second World War? Is it, in fact, a term made racist by its use in post-war Australia? Academics have recently argued that 'wog' has an entirely separate, older derivation entirely free of racialised connotations.

Of course, the somewhat geeky etymological debates and contests over exact historical origins miss the point. The meanings associated with the golliwog are not frozen to a particular time. In the decades following the Second World War, racism became an increasingly virulent social force in Britain. When children were reading Enid Blyton books in the 1950s and 60s, her descriptions of golliwog characters resonated with the everyday racism of those times. By highlighting the following extract from *The Three Golliwogs*, published in 1944, we could easily argue that the *racist* 'origins' for the golliwog re-start here afresh:

> Once the three bold Golliwogs, Golly, Woggie, and Nigger, decided to go for a walk to Bumble-Bee Common. Golly wasn't quite ready so Woggie and Nigger said they would start off without him, and Golly would catch them up as soon as he could. So off went Woggie and Nigger, arm-in-arm, singing merrily their favourite song — which, as you may guess, was 'Ten Little Nigger Boys'.

The 'racist' significance of images, words and objects should depend on what's going on in the world outside. Today, controversies over golliwogs exist in an entirely new context — not of racism, but of racial etiquette. This is a culture of offence-taking and fear of giving offence which, at its most febrile, imagines the image of the golliwog (or simply the utterance of the g-word) to transmit racism all by itself.

In this conception, images, words and objects are fixed and held captive by the historical origins they are presumed to have. At worst they become invested with near-magical qualities similar to a sacred (or perhaps cursed) relic or talisman possessing the power to transmit good or evil. That such eccentricity can afflict some of us points directly to the fashionable, post-Macpherson, psychologised view of racism as something unwitting or unconscious which can be triggered or incited by external forces — even objects or word-sounds, which are themselves considered so intrinsically offensive that they have the power to inflict emotional injury.

But more telling is the fact that most of us would indeed wince at the sight of a shop window full of golliwogs. We wince, not necessarily because we think the dolls are shooting evil spells out into the high street, inciting racists and injuring black identity, but rather because we know we have strayed upon an act of modern-day heresy which could taint us by association.

When I began writing this book late in 2013, stories concerning racist golliwogs were coming thick and fast. One of these concerned the long, drawn-out tribunal case, finally reaching a conclusion, of an assistant chef at the London School of Economics (LSE) who had been offended by her chef manager's utterance of the word 'golliwog'.[17] In 2009, Chef Mark McAleese had allegedly used the word 'golliwog' in the course of an informal workplace conversation about food labelling with his black colleague Denise Lindsay. His conversation had strayed onto the controversy surrounding the notorious 'golliwog' logo that was once used by Robertsons Jam.[18] Lindsay's complaint to the LSE at being subjected to the word *golliwog* had initially resulted in an apology from McAleese, along with his agreement to attend diversity training, but later resulted in Lindsay making a claim of racial harassment to the courts.

Lord Justice Floyd, sitting in the Court of Appeal, upheld the ruling of racial harassment stating that the term 'golliwog', said in front of a black person and regardless of context, was 'obviously racist and offensive'.[19] For McAleese, any hope of appealing to context quickly evaporated when he appeared to agree that such an act would be 'downright offensive'. Moreover, at the time of the alleged offence (some four years earlier), it seems he had been inconsistent over whether he'd said the g-word at all, first admitting it and dutifully attending diversity training but later denying saying the g-word at all. With Lord Justice Floyd accepting that any use of the term 'golliwog' in conversation with a black person is offensive, McAleese's opportunity to mitigate his racial insensitivity by claiming it was unwitting was squandered. It was a word, said the judge, that McAleese 'recognised could cause serious offence'.[20]

In the future, it seems, it will be hard for anyone to claim that they were not aware of a word's potential to offend (our conversations will need to steer around them). The case shows us that British courts are willing to view the word 'golliwog' as inherently offensive and defendants can only hope that they provide a convincing excuse for its innocent use.

But what about the *inherent racism* of the golliwog image itself? This became the theme of another golliwog headline, also from late 2013.[21] Here, a primary school's Alice in Wonderland wall mural, painted in 1936, which contained a small golliwog image in one corner, had been reported to police as a 'hate incident'. The victim of the incident had been a mother touring the Edinburgh school with a view to sending her child there.

Margaret Neizer-Rocha contacted police and local councillors after spotting the golliwog in the far corner of one of the mural panels some 20 feet above the school's gymnasium floor. Mrs Rocha said she found the image 'deeply offensive' and would not be sending her son to the school. 'It's one thing if it was a museum piece or an art exhibition, where you might explain what a swastika was or a Ku Klux Klan outfit', said Rocha, who argued that the golliwog image 'goes back to the American Black Sambo — the blacked-up face. It's offensive to me. I find it racially offensive'.[22]

In the event, the police investigation into the incident was dropped, and discussions over removing or covering up the golliwog switched to a commitment from the school to continue to use the mural in a positive way as an anti-racism educational resource. For a while though, as police liaised with Edinburgh's education department over what to do and the story hit the national media, the prospect of the school being forced to remove the offending image seemed eminently possible. Even the Heritage Lottery Fund, which had recently funded the mural's restoration, confirmed that it was in touch with the school on how best to proceed.[23]

The school mural saga shows us how easy it is for offence-takers to cry 'that's racist!', trigger police investigations and excitable press reporting and—in this instance—very nearly force the censorship of an artwork of some historical significance. Indeed, it is a sign of the times that it took 78 years for this particular golliwog to commit a hate incident.

Yet another example of late 2013's open season on golliwogs took place in my hometown of Brighton. It began with the predictable offence-taker complaint, this time over retro 'Robertson Jam' coasters featuring a picnic scene (attended, of course, by the hapless golliwog). The coasters were discovered on sale in the gifts and novelties shop *Bert's Homestore*, and it would appear that the offence-taker contacted the local paper. The paper then contacted 72-year-old local councillor Dawn Barnett for comment, whereupon Barnett stated her opinion that golliwogs 'are nostalgic, not racist'.

In the article, headlined 'Councillor Backs Golliwog Sales in Brighton Shop', the *Argus* reporter quotes one anti-racism campaigner describing golliwogs as 'a sick throwback' that should be banned.[24] Quoting Abigail Sinclair (whom we met during the Varndean scandal, above), the article states '[Sinclair] who campaigns for community cohesion in Brighton and Hove, said pictures of golliwogs had "no place" in the city. She said: "I was called a golliwog as a kid so it's very offensive to me. It's not something that belongs in the present day"'.[25] Cllr Barnett's published comments immediately triggered a fresh wave of offence-takers to issue official complaints to the council.

According to the council, it received 'four separate but very similar complaints about statements made by Councillor Barnett' from one council tenant, two council workers and the council's Black and Minority Ethnic Workers' Forum (BMEWF).[26] One of the individual complainants wrote: 'what I would like to see happen is that Ms Barnett is expelled without

further delay for her reckless and irresponsible comments
which have directly led to racial tension, antagonism and dis-
harmony in my personal life', and added that he had 'raised a
Police Incident against Ms Barnett'.[27] The two other individual
complainants demanded that Cllr Barnett attend compulsory
diversity training.

All four complaints led to an extensive investigation by the
council's standards committee and a 70-page internal report on
its findings.[28] Cllr Barnett was ordered to attend a Standards
Hearing (which are open to the public) and, after the first was
deemed so rowdy police had to be called, a second 'closed'
hearing found her guilty of bringing the council into disrepute.[29]
The report and details of the hearing's findings were placed on
the Council's website but then removed. Fortunately a saved
copy made its way to an online blog.[30]

In its report, the standards committee stated that Cllr
Barnett's 'support for and encouragement for the continued sale
of golliwogs, instead of fostering good relations between people
who share a protected characteristic and those who do not, had
the potential to cause division and offend some sections of the
community'.[31] The committee's findings also stated that 'The
Council has given a commitment to zero tolerance of racist
attitudes and behaviours. Councillor Barnett's statements to the
newspaper are not consistent with these requirements'.[32] Of
some consolation to Cllr Barnett was the police's decision that
'there was insufficient admissible evidence to show that
Councillor Barnett intended that her comments should stir up
racial hatred, or that she could have expected that racial hatred
was likely to be stirred up by her comments'.[33]

The Brighton *Argus* reports that, as part of the hearing's
decision, the panel 'recommended that all 54 councillors attend
diversity workshops'.[34] The workshops took place in April 2014,
with the first session billed as follows: 'This session will explore
the terminology that is used to describe aspects of difference.
We will discuss the impact of language and how it can influence
our understanding of "difference" as compared with "norm-
ality". Why are some terms loaded with negative meaning?

And what makes a particular term acceptable? The session will give an overview of the protected characteristics under the Equalities Act, 2010 and we will discuss how we can recognise and challenge discrimination.' One letter to the *Argus* neatly sums up the logic of a rule-book that demands total conformity of thought and expression from elected representatives: 'Do experienced councillors really need to be told what to think? If so, why do we bother voting them in? Why aren't they just appointed?'[35]

Case 3: Kicking 'racist' footballers

Played out across the world's media, the accusation that British football is shot through with racism kicked off in October 2011, and remained the preoccupation of the political and football elite for most of the following year. The incident that provided the most enduring symbol of football's modern malaise concerned the Chelsea defender and England captain John Terry, who allegedly racially abused Anton Ferdinand mid-match with the words 'fucking black cunt'. Coming just days after another incident—this time involving Liverpool player Luis Suarez calling Manchester United's Patrice Evra 'negrito'—the issue of racism in football quickly gained continuous media attention.

Although both Suarez and Terry argued that the *context* of the incidents needed to be taken into account, the Football Association's (FA) anti-racist charity Kick it Out had, by this time, played a decisive role in trumping any discussion on context by continually invoking 'zero tolerance'. By rallying opinion around the need for a righteous, unequivocal condemnation of the evil of racism, anything less than an ostentatious, zero tolerance declaration of anti-racist *goodthinking* was to fall wantonly short.

A spectacular example of such failure came in the form of Sepp Blatter, president of the international football association FIFA. When, just a few weeks after the Suarez/Terry incidents, Blatter argued on CNN that on-pitch spats between players ought to be resolved with a handshake, Kick it Out chair

Herman Ouseley was incensed. 'He has no understanding of what racism is, the ideology behind it, the damage it causes and how it subjugates one group of people as inferior. Minor matters on the field often can be resolved with a handshake', said Ouseley. 'Racism is not a minor matter.'[36]

From denunciations instantly tweeted by David Beckham and Rio Ferdinand to the official statements hurriedly issued by Prime Minister David Cameron and Opposition leader Ed Milliband, calls for Blatter's resignation rolled in from every corner. Indeed, for public figures, failing to voice anti-racist indignation about these incidents became unthinkable. Cameron's statement affirmed: 'it's appalling to suggest that racism in any way should be accepted as part of the game.' A parliamentary Early Day Motion signed by 59 MPs and lobbied for by the schools charity Show Racism the Red Card copied Ouseley's words verbatim: '[The President of FIFA]... has no understanding of what racism is, the ideology behind it, the damage it causes and how it subjugates one group of people as inferior...'[37] In this, and almost every other statement appeared the phrase 'zero tolerance'.

Blatter eventually recanted his sins, giving an interview with BBC Sport in which he said he 'deeply regretted' his 'unfortunate words'.[38] 'Blatter now says any players found guilty of racism on the pitch should be thrown out of the game', reported the *Independent*. 'This was a good lesson for me as well', said Blatter, 'It should be and shall be zero tolerance'.[39] The FA later punished Suarez and Terry: for Terry, this meant a four match ban and a £220,000 fine. But even as Blatter recanted, a hate-incident complaint made to Scotland Yard by an off-duty police-man offended either by the match or the relevant YouTube clip led to John Terry becoming the first player to face a criminal charge of racial abuse.[40] The complainant was, perhaps, the first case of a person racially offended via his own or others' lip-reading skills.

Whether or not we approve of the warlike, adrenaline-fuelled game of professional league football or the unbridled passions of its fans, even the most vociferous advocates of zero tolerance might still, in private, quietly agree with sport's unwritten code: the adage, 'what's said on the pitch should stay on the pitch' (and be resolved at the end with a handshake). The sports columnist Duleep Allirajah argues that on-pitch abuse and 'sledging' (provoking opponents by striking a raw nerve) has, for years, been accepted and tolerated in football precisely because its context is understood. 'This isn't genteel Radio 4 repartee,' says Allirajah, 'it's war minus the shooting… Yes, you need a thick skin, but the rules of engagement are fairly clear – or at least they used to be.'[41] Even the prosecuting barrister in the Terry case noted that if a red card were given every time the word 'cunt' was yelled, the game would be unlikely to last more than 10 minutes.[42]

We might also apply this point to the fans on the terraces, who have long since known that to engage in full-blooded displays of disrespect for their rivals is a 90-minute ritual. As journalist and avid Manchester United fan Mick Hume notes, 'football is not played in a courtroom or at a supper party. It involves the unleashing of passions and conflicts that can burst out in all kinds of unpredictable directions, yet can fade and disappear again just as quickly once the match is over'.[43]

Interestingly, most of those who had loudly condemned Blatter and called for zero tolerance towards Terry and Suarez took care to acknowledge that football's record on racism had, along with society itself, changed immeasurably. And few wanted to suggest that Suarez or Terry were actually 'racists'. John Barnes, the former England international and patron of Show Racism the Red Card, who remembers football's bad old days only too well, was later to say: 'I would never, ever say John Terry was a racist.' Qualifying his remark, Barnes went on to describe Terry as 'no more or less racist than anyone else', adding that 99 percent of us 'are unconscious racists'.[44]

In February 2012, news services reported from a special Downing Street summit on the crisis facing football, called by David Cameron. With John Barnes sat at his side, Cameron told reporters, 'What happens on the field influences what happens off the field. You see children as young as six imitating the behaviour they see'. 'We need to act quickly to make sure those problems do not creep back in', he added.[45]

The following month, Bolton Wanderers midfielder Fabrice Muamba suffered a cardiac arrest during a televised FA Cup match with Tottenham Hotspur. A wave of shock and com-,passion for Muamba engulfed the watching crowds and fans everywhere. Although Muamba survived, the shocking event was eclipsed by reports that a drunk Swansea University student had tweeted odious and racist comments about Muamba to his 300 followers. The first of his tweets read, 'LOL. Fuck Muamba. He's dead!'[46]

In a Twittersphere awash with 340 million tweets a day, it took just a few offended recipients passing on their outrage and issuing complaints to the police to ensure that the culprit, 21-year-old Liam Stacey, became a national hate figure. Stacey's arrest came after news of his offensive tweets reached England international Stan Collymore, who made his own complaint to the police. Less than two weeks later, Stacey was jailed for 56 days after admitting a racially aggravated public disorder offence.

Summing up, the judge told Stacey that his hateful tweets had come at a moment when Muamba's family, the footballing world and the whole world were praying for Fabrice's life; and 'your comments aggravated this situation'.[47] The news of Stacey's custodial sentence garnered instant approval, ranging from *Apprentice* star Lord Alan Sugar tweeting 'BLOODY GOOD JOB. Be warned idiots!', to others tweeting that they hoped inmates would 'rape the fuck out of him' in prison, '#DONTDROPTHESOAP', and that 'I wouldn't really care if Liam Stacey died. He's a sick man, from the scum of the earth'.[48]

On 13 July 2012, John Terry was cleared at Westminster Magistrates Court of racially insulting Anton Ferdinand. In a court of law where establishing context and intent is (usually) relevant, it had proved impossible to determine the nature of the incident. The verdict unleashed fury amongst those for whom only a 'guilty' verdict could have served the anti-racist cause. Terry had argued that he had merely repeated back words he thought had been 'sledged' at him, but this, apparently, was irrelevant: he had admitted speaking the words. 'Many fear it will take us back to the dark days of the 1980s when racial abuse was rife', commented ex-player Garth Crooks.[49] Former basketball player John Amaechi described the verdict as a travesty. 'Thanks football', he tweeted. 'You set the entire country back a decade... "black cunt" now officially ok to say.'[50]

Writing in the *Times*, Duwayne Brooks, who had been with Stephen Lawrence on the night of his murder, argued that 'a guilty verdict would have been a breath of fresh air for football'.[51] Hints that the John Terry case had more than a passing connection with the murder of Stephen Lawrence took different forms. From inside the Terry trial courtroom, one *Guardian* reporter spotted 'a quiet dignified' Doreen Lawrence, who was watching the proceedings, he presumed, 'to see if another race-related crime had been committed'.[52] Although the reporter was careful to add that this alleged crime was 'albeit a much less serious one', the febrile atmosphere that had built up by summer 2012 made for easy comparisons between the likes of Terry and the Lawrence murder suspects.

For many, Terry conformed exactly to an image of working-class white boy turned upstart millionaire; 'chavvy' and badly behaved. Once regarded as such, he was a walking racial stereo-type for middle-class lynch mobs to pronounce 'probably guilty anyway'. As the *Guardian* reporter approvingly noted of the court proceedings, football had been rightly exposed as vicious, vulgar and foul-mouthed. In the sober surroundings of the courtroom, Terry's attempt to explain the ubiquitous practice of sledging 'brought home just how trashy and puerile it all was'.[53] Terry had tried to explain the ritualised blunt irreverence of fan chants too, much to the incredulity of the court... and the reporter. 'The average football match was depicted as a hateful place', said the reporter, 'where crowds look for weakness and attack with a zombie mentality.'

The comparison with the Lawrence murder, implicit in such genteel misinterpretations of the working-class experience of football, was that the gap between offensive language and murder was not that great. Not only could words be imagined as so hate-fuelled that their offensiveness cut the psyche of victims like a knife: once uttered, the words provided a potential trigger for barely contained zombie-like savagery.

In the space of just 12 months, beginning with the Suarez and Terry incidents in October 2011, claims about the ubiquitous character of 'racism in football' had reached their peak. John Terry's FA hearing in September 2012 was a belated victory for those who were by now desperate for an example-setting conclusion to their campaign for zero tolerance. The fact that the FA's disciplinary hearing, unencumbered by rules of evidence, could draw the conclusion that Terry was in fact guilty delighted campaign groups such as Kick it Out and Show Racism the Red Card. For Herman Ouseley, the length of time taken to get to this hearing indicated the FA's failure of moral leadership. Speaking on BBC Radio 4's *Today* programme in December 2012, Ouseley complained that the clubs 'should be setting that moral tone in saying "we have an employee who's behaving quite outrageously and we're going to do something about him", but they don't do that, they say *"no, that person's innocent until proved guilty"'*.[54]

For Macpherson-inspired anti-racist campaigners, the instantaneous 'guilty' judgment conferred by an approach of zero tolerance has little to do with the rules of courtrooms or even FA hearings. As Ouseley's comments indicate, the point of such hearings is less to punish or exonerate individuals than it is to attack racism immediately in whatever ugly form it manifests itself. Arguments over intention, context and individual guilt come to be seen as irrelevant. As one sports writer on the site FootballSpeak expressed it: '[A]s long as humans continue to be born, racism will be a problem. The process of conquering it is continuous and never-ending.'[55]

In one final incident from that year-long catalogue of racism-in-football incidents, the manifestation of racism's evil turned out to be less clear cut. In October 2012, Chelsea tried to demonstrate text-book official anti-racism when it demanded the FA investigate allegations that referee Mark Clattenburg racially abused midfielder John Obi Mikel with the term 'monkey'. Chelsea dutifully applied the Macpherson definition of a racist incident as 'any incident perceived to be racist by the victim or any other person'. The alleged victim, Mikel, hadn't heard anything, but *'any other person'*—in the form of Chelsea's Brazilian midfielder Ramires—had. Keen to do its best to demonstrate efficient official anti-racism, the FA conducted a prompt, exhaustive investigation and, a month later, concluded there was no evidence to support the allegation.

Ramires, who was standing 10 yards away from Clattenburg, amidst the roar of 40,000 fans, is now thought to have imagined 'monkey' from Clattenburg's north-east pronunciation of 'mikel'.[56]

By the time Clattenburg was cleared by the FA, the efforts of anti-racist campaigners to instigate police proceedings against him had also floundered. The press frenzy over Mikel's 'monkey' allegation had been enough to inspire Peter Herbert of the Society for Black Lawyers (SBL) to report Clattenburg to the police. Scotland Yard dutifully opened proceedings—presumably based on Herbert's perception of Clattenburg's racism via press coverage—but found nobody willing to cooperate.[57]

Furious that Chelsea FC and the FA had not supported his police complaint, Herbert said: '[T]he FA is institutionally racist, has not got a handle on this issue, and its refusal to report this matter to the police looks like it is one of those football cover-ups.'[58] When quizzed by *Sky Sports News* over his comments about the FA, Herbert said, 'Institutionally racist? Of course it is. They don't even implement what the Stephen Lawrence Inquiry recommendations were about, how to report a racial incident, whether the victim or any other person believes it is'.[59]

The Mark Clattenburg debacle provided the first instance in which a seemingly unstoppable assault on racism in football faltered. On the FA's resolution of the Clattenburg case, Herman Ouseley tried to sound undaunted, stating that 'irrespective of today's outcome, the message remains clear: report perceived abuse, whether seen or heard, to the relevant authorities for the required process to take place'.[60] But several leading advocates of zero tolerance appeared to flinch at how 'perceived abuse' and 'required process' had almost destroyed a career. Clarke Carlisle, a vocal anti-racist and chair of the Professional Footballers' Association (PFA), could not contain his irritation with Herbert: '[he] is speaking about this incident from a position of little or zero evidence.'[61] And by now the emphatic line adopted by former and current black players over racism in football had already wavered.

Only weeks earlier, the former England goalkeeper David James accused anti-racist groups of hyping-up the problem to justify their existence. In a veiled reference to Kick it Out, 'some people' in 'certain jobs', said James, had 'an agenda to keep themselves in existence and, as a [black] player, I don't see the racism issue — anywhere'.[62] Newspaper sports writers were now openly contemptuous of 'racism in football' claims-makers. Martin Samuel mocked the 'steady drip of innuendo' across the year 'from those who haven't a genuine clue either way'.[63] Terry, Suarez and 'that guy in the crowd at Chelsea', says Samuel, 'and... some quite nasty individuals on Twitter... are all packaged together, these lone souls, into a festering boil called *Racism in Football*'. Then there was the embarrassment of February 2013, when former player and Kick it Out trustee Paul Elliot texted, 'Ur a stupid man nigger...' to another black former player.[64] Elliot was duly excommunicated from the anti-racist circle.

Conclusion: the monitor within

Despite the occasional backlash against 'anti-racism gone mad', the censorious etiquette promoted by anti-racist policies is now more ingrained than ever. As the sociologist Stuart Waiton wrote in *The Scotsman* in 2012, 'it is not possible to mix in the right circles today without being a card-carrying official anti-racist'.[65] A veteran anti-racist campaigner himself, Waiton neatly describes the tragedy of the modern offence-seeking version, which results in relations between black and white made 'distant, awkward and confused'. Such a climate of hypersensitivity, says Waiton, 'turns even the most anti-racist individual into an anxious, tongue-twisted twerp, unable to have a conversation with a colleague without feeling the need to receive linguistic correctness training, just in case'.

After Reginald D. Hunter's n-word littered performance at the PFA Awards Dinner,[66] discussed in the previous chapter, 'anxious' and 'unable to have a conversation' may have well described how FA chairman David Bernstein felt. Journalist Martin Samuel noted that Bernstein 'scuttled away refusing to comment'. For the despairing Samuel, Bernstein was illustrative of a sport now inextricably stuck inside its own moral minefield: 'we are at a dead end with our perception of ethical principle. We do not know where to turn, we cannot retrace our steps, we see no way out.'[67] 'Legislation can help [tackle] overt racism, racist chanting in grounds', says John Barnes, but 'all you do then is keep your mouth shut, you can be as racist in thought as you like. I'm interested in getting rid of the racist thoughts'.[68] 'What we have to attack', says Clarke Carlisle, 'is base level language use and opinion… and that means we have to re-educate our youngsters so they know what is acceptable.'[69]

In November 2012, on Eddie Nestor's BBC Radio London *Drivetime* show, I discussed the topic of 'racism and children' with Lord Herman Ouseley.[70] Ouseley was eager to agree with me that kids should not be labelled as 'racists' for behaving childishly, but seemed convinced that their racist *language* stemmed from the influence of parents at home and the racism that was 'part of life'. For Ouseley, eliminating racism was, apparently, all about snuffing out 'unacceptable' language and breaking its power to transmit what Macpherson had dubbed as the 'disease' of racism.

And so here we have the vision of racism, and anti-racism, in 2014. Racism has become detached from actions and intentions; it is seen to be everywhere, but its meaning is contested and confused. Meanwhile the anti-racist utopia that campaigners vigorously try to construct on the foundations of speech codes and policies is one in which individuals are continually trying, and failing, to adopt correct attitudes. They end up 'anxious, tongue-twisted twerps', who dance around each other in their vain attempts not to cause offence.

Endnotes:

1   See: Institute for Race Relations news-page at: http://www.irr.org. uk/themes/education/news/page/5/; and ICARE 'hate crime news' at: http://www.icare.to/article.php?id=40006&lang=en. Accessed 17 May 2014.

2   Gardner, B. (2012) 'Brighton Schoolgirl Hounded by Racist Bullies', *The Argus*, 4 July. Accessed 17 May 2014. Available at: http://www. theargus.co.uk/news/9797373.Brighton_schoolgirl_hounded_by_ racist_bullies/

3   Gardner, B. (2012) 'Racism Probe at Varndean School', *The Argus*, 8 July. Accessed 17 May 2014. Available at: http://www.theargus.co. uk/news/9805098.Racism_probe_at_Varndean_school_in_Brighton /

4   As of 17 May 2014 a Google search on 'racist bullying in UK schools' brings up this story on page 6 of approximately 4,970,000 results.

5   See: This is Bristol (2009) 'Southmead Police and Residents Hit Back at BBC Panorama "Racism" Claims', *Bristol Post,* 21 October. Accessed 21 May 2014. Available at: http://www.bristolpost.co.uk/ Southmead-police-residents-hit-BBC-Panorama-racism-claims/ story-11301065-detail/story.html

6   Gardner, B. (2012) 'Racism Probe at Brighton School', *The Argus*, 8 July. Accessed 17 May 2014. Available at: http://www.theargus.co. uk/news/9805098.Racism_probe_at_Varndean_school_in_Brighton /

7   Mosaic is a 'third sector' partner of Brighton and Hove Council. Its website states: 'MOSAIC is the only resource which exists in Brighton & Hove and Sussex to combat racism specifically within the Black and mixed-parentage community.' See: http://www. mosaicequalities.org.uk/homepage-page/2/page/index.html. Accessed 18 May 2014.

8   Email from Councillor Sue Shanks, Chair of Children and Young People Committee, 24 October 2013.

9   Emailed response to FOI request 27 January 2014.

10 See: Brighton & Hove City Council (2012) 'Bullying and Prejudice-Based Incident Recording and Reporting Guidance for Brighton & Hove Schools'. Accessed 17 May 2014. Available at: http://present. brighton-hove.gov.uk/Published/C00000835/M00004862/ AI00034737/$5BHreportingguidanceV3Jan2013fromSamBeal.pdfA. ps.pdf

11 As of 31 August 2013 Varndean had 1336 pupils of which 1007 were recorded on roll as 'White—British'.

12 Jasper, L. (2011) 'Why Golliwog Wars are Important', Lee Jasper's

official blog, 6 October. Accessed 18 May 2014. Available at: http://leejasper.blogspot.co.uk/2011/10/why-golliwog-wars-are-important.html

13 Upton, B., with illustrations by Upton, F.K. (1895) *The Adventures of Two Dutch Dolls and a Golliwogg*, London: Longman's Green & Co. To see an e-book version in full go to: http://www.gutenberg.org/files/16770/16770-h/16770-h.htm. Accessed 18 May 2014.

14 There is indeed an illustration of a black-faced minstrel half way through the Upton book, playing a banjo and accompanied by the words 'sambo plays a song'.

15 Henley, J. (2009) 'From Bedtime Story to Ugly Insult: How Victorian Caricature Became a Racial Slur', *Guardian*, 6 February. Accessed 18 May 2014. Available at: http://www.theguardian.com/media/2009/feb/06/race-thatcher-golliwog. Also see: Pilgrim, D. (2000) 'The Golliwog Caricature', *Jim Crow Museum of Racist Memorabilia*. Accessed 18 May 2014. Available at: http://www.ferris.edu/jimcrow/golliwog/

16 *Ibid.*

17 Carter, C. (2013) 'Discussing Robertson's Jam "Golliwog" Label is Racist, Judge Rules', *Daily Telegraph*, 18 December. Accessed 18 May 2014. Available at: http://www.telegraph.co.uk/news/uknews/law-and-order/10525121/Discussing-Robertsons-jam-golliwog-label-is-racist-judge-rules.html

18 James Robertson & Sons, a manufacturer of jams and preserves, began using the Golliwog as its trademark in the early 1900s. Known only as 'the Golly', the image appeared on Robertson's product labels and price lists. Its popularity led to a mail-order campaign where, in return for coupons from the jam-jars, Robertson's sent Golly brooches and, by the 1960s, musician figurines.

19 *Ibid.*

20 De Peyer, R. (2013) 'LSE Chef's "Gollywog" Jam Reference in Front of Black Colleague Held to be Harassment', *Evening Standard*, 19 December. Accessed 18 May 2014. Available at: http://www.standard.co.uk/news/uk/lse-chefs-gollywog-jam-reference-in-front-of-black-colleague-held-to-be-harassment-9013470.html

21 Grant, G. (2013) 'The Mural Lovingly Restored for Primary School Children but Now at Centre of Hate Complaint', *The Daily Mail*, 19 November. Accessed 18 March 2014. Available at: http://www.dailymail.co.uk/news/article-2509722/The-mural-lovingly-restored-primary-children-centre-hate-complaint.html

22 Carrell, S. (2013) 'Edinburgh Council Refuses to Cover Up Golliwog Image on School Wall Mural', *Guardian*, 17 November. Accessed 18 May 2014. Available at: http://www.theguardian.com/uk-news/2013/nov/17/edinburgh-council-refuses-golliwog-school-racism

23 *Ibid.*

24 Gardner, B. (2013) 'Councillor Backs Golliwog Sales in Brighton Shop', *The Argus*, 30 August. Accessed 18 May 2014. Available at: http://www.theargus.co.uk/news/10643948.Councillor_backs_golliwog_sales_in_Brighton_shop/

25 *Ibid.*

26 You can read the council's report here: http://brightonbygolly.files.wordpress.com/2013/12/dawn-barnett-standards-agenda-28-11-13.pdf. It combines the Standards Committee's final decision, made on 28 November 2013, with the Investigation Report dated 19 November 2013, which states: 'This Report represents the final findings of an investigation carried out under the Brighton & Hove City Council arrangements for dealing with allegations of breaches of the Members' Code of Conduct under the Localism Act 2011. The investigation has been carried out by … [the] Standards and Complaints Manager, on behalf of the Monitoring Officer for Brighton & Hove City Council into an allegation concerning Councillor Dawn Barnett and is to be presented to a Hearing Panel of the Audit and Standards Committee' (p5).

27 *Ibid.*, p27.

28 Brighton & Hove City Council (2013) 'Standard's Committee Final Report — Complaints about Councillor Dawn Barnett's Comments in a Local Newspaper', 19 November, p5. Accessed 21 May 2014. Available at: http://brightonbygolly.files.wordpress.com

29 See: *Brighton & Hove News* (2013) 'Councillor Found Guilty of Misconduct for Saying Golliwogs Are Not Racist', 19 December. Accessed 18 May 2014. Available at: http://www.brightonandhovenews.org/2013/12/19/councillor-found-guilty-of-misconduct-for-saying-gollwogs-are-not-racist/26080/comment-page-1

Not only did police cars arrive at hearing chambers, ambulances did too — while on the phone to her lawyer Cllr Barnett slipped and fell down the stairs. Although finding her guilty of bringing the council into disrepute, the hearing cleared Cllr Barnett of two other alleged breaches of the code of conduct for members: (a) 'You must treat others with respect', and (b) 'You must not do anything which may cause your authority to breach any of its equality duties (in particular as set out in the Equality Act 2010)'. In addition to Cllr Barnett's apparent failure to understand that golliwogs *are* racist, her press comment that banning the sale of the offending items was 'political correctness gone too far' was itself deemed as offensive and a failure in her 'moral duty to foster good relations…'. Direct evidence of racial division was deduced from the number of comments placed under the *Argus* article which demonstrated, claimed the council's investigation report, 'divided opinion' over the matter of political correctness. Members of the public who merely supported Barnett's view were thus regarded — somewhat bizarrely — as evi-

30   See: http://brightonbygolly.files.wordpress.com. Accessed 14 June
     2014.
31   Brighton & Hove City Council (2013) 'Hearing of Allegation that a
     Councillor has Failed to Comply with the Code of Conduct for
     Members — Cases BHC–012702, 012751, 012777, 012843', 28
     November, p2. Accessed 21 May 2014. Available at: http://
     brightonbygolly.files.wordpress.com/2013/12/dawn-barnett-
     standards-agenda-28-11-13.pdf
32   *Ibid.*
33   Brighton & Hove City Council (2013) 'Standard's Committee Final
     Report — Complaints about Councillor Dawn Barnett's Comments in
     a Local Newspaper', p67. Accessed 21 May 2014. Available at:
     http:// brightonbygolly.files.wordpress.com/2013/12/dawn-
     barnett-standards-agenda-28-11-13.pdf

dence of an erosion of good race relations.

One of the issues considered by Sussex Police was whether Cllr Barnett's comments amounted to the offence of incitement to racial hatred within the meaning of that expression under section 18 of the Public Order Act 1986. This states: 'A person who uses threatening, abusive or insulting words or behaviour, or displays any written material which is threatening, abusive or insulting, is guilty of an offence if: (a) they intend thereby to stir up racial hatred, or (b) having regard to all the circumstances racial hatred is likely to be stirred up thereby.' Also see pp25–41: one of the four complainants (who had also logged hate incidents against Cllr Barnett and *Bert's Homestore* with the police), argued that Cllr Barnett had incited racial hatred toward the black and Asian community by describing the original complaints to *Bert's Homestore* as 'political correctness' and thus stirring hatred toward the black and British Asian community 'because it was we who complained to Bert's store about the Golliwog image they stocked'. Exploiting the public's irritation over examples of 'political correctness' in order that they take sides against the black community was, suggests the complainant, Cllr Barnett's objective. 'I perceive…', says the complainant, 'the Councillor's true intention was to incite and create racial tension in the community over this matter.' He goes on to argue that the comments posted under the *Argus* article prove his claim, including posts 'which directly abused the good name and honourable work of Ms Abigail Sinclair, who works in the Community with Black and British Asian people… Dawn Barnett's comments have therefore directly incited hatred and abuse towards a good citizen of the Brighton and Hove Community who does exceptional work'. I couldn't find any posts (there were 140) that were unduly abusive toward Sinclair unless 'dimwit' counts? 'Abigail Sinclair "campaigns for community cohesion" funniest thing I have read in ages!! If dim-

wits like these hadn't pointed out the "racist" thing no-one would
have noticed!'

34 Vowels, N. (2014) 'Former Policeman Calls for Judicial Review into
     Brighton and Hove Golliwog Row', 04 February. Accessed 16 May
     2014. Available at: http://www.theargus.co.uk/news/10983941.
     Former_policeman_calls_for_judicial_review_into_Brighton_and_
     Hove_golliwog_row/

35 See the *Argus* letters page (2014) 'Equalities Training for Councillors:
     For and Against', 29 January. Accessed 18 May 2014. Available at:
     http://www.theargus.co.uk/opinion/letters/10969051.Equalities_
     training_for_councillors___for_and_against/

36 Gibsin, O. (2011) 'Sepp Blatter Uses Twitter to Hit Back at Criticism
     of Remarks on Racism', *Guardian*, 17 November. Accessed 18 May
     2014. Available at: http://www.theguardian.com/football/2011/
     nov/17/sepp-blatter-racism-rio-ferdinand

37 Early Day Motion 2444: SEPP BLATTER. Session: 2010–12; Date
     tabled: 21.11.2011; Primary sponsor: Anderson, David. Accessed 18
     May 2014. Available at: http://www.parliament.uk/edm/2010-
     12/2444

38 BBC Sport (2011) 'Sepp Blatter Says Sorry for Comments on Racism',
     BBC Sport, 18 November. Accessed 18 May 2014. Available at:
     http://www.bbc.co.uk/sport/0/football/15782265

39 *Independent* (2011) 'Sepp Blatter Says Sorry for Racism Remarks',
     Independent, 18 November. Accessed 18 May 2014. Available at:
     http://www.independent.co.uk/sport/football/news-and-
     comment/sepp-blatter-says-sorry-for-racism-remarks-6264229.html

40 Longman, J. (2011) 'Racism Charges Put a Sport on Edge', *New York
     Times*, 21 December. Accessed 18 May 2014. Available at: http://
     www.nytimes.com/2011/12/22/sports/soccer/in-england-star-
     players-accused-of-racist-comments.html.

41 Allirajah, D. (2011) 'What's Said on the Pitch Should Stay on the
     Pitch', *Spiked*, 4 November. Accessed 18 May 2014. Available at:
     http://www.spiked-online.com/newsite/article/11373#.
     U3i51NJdXfK

42 Taylor, D. (2012) 'John Terry is Cleared but Football's Reputation
     Takes a Battering', *Guardian*, 13 July. Accessed 18 May 2014. Avail-
     able at: http://www.theguardian.com/football/2012/jul/13/john-
     terry-cleared-football-reputation

43 Hume, M. (2012) 'John Terry — and Football — Found Guilty Any-
     way', *Spiked*, 16 July. Accessed 18 May 2014. Available at: http://
     www.spiked-online.com/newsite/article/12646#.U3i_zNJdXfJ

44 Moore, G., and Wallace, S. (2012) 'John Barnes: John Terry is Guilty
     of "Unconscious Racism"', *Independent*, 28 September. Accessed 18
     May 2014. Available at: http://www.independent.co.uk/sport/
     football/news-and-comment/john-barnes-john-terry-is-guilty-of-

unconscious-racism-8182579.html

45 Churcher, J. (2012) 'Football Must "Crush" Racism Says Prime
    Minister', *Independent*, 22 February. Accessed 18 May. Available at:
    http://www.independent.co.uk/sport/football/news-and-
    comment/football-must-crush-racism-says-prime-minister-
    7298196.html

46 Morris, S. (2012) 'Student Who Mocked Fabrice Muamba on Twitter
    "Massively Sorry"', *Guardian*, 22 May. Accessed 21 May 2014.
    Available at: http://www.theguardian.com/uk/2012/may/22/
    muamba-twitter-abuse-student-sorry

47 *Ibid.*

48 See: Pilditch, D. (2012) 'Sobbing Student Sent to Jail in Cuffs for
    "Vile" Muamba Twitter Rant', *Daily Express*, 28 March. Accessed 18
    May 2014. Available at: http://www.express.co.uk/news/uk/
    310955/Sobbing-student-sent-to-jail-in-cuffs-for-vile-Muamba-
    Twitter-rant

49 Crooks, G. (2012) 'John Terry Trial: Now the FA Must Act', *Guardian*,
    13 July. Accessed 18 May 2014. Available at: http://www.
    theguardian.com/commentisfree/2012/jul/13/john-terry-trial-fa

50 Hytner, D. (2012) 'John Terry Verdict Angers Black Players',
    Guardian, 13 July. Accessed 18 May 2014. Available at: http://www.
    theguardian.com/football/2012/jul/13/john-terry-verdict-angers-
    black-players

51 Hume, M. (2012) *Op. cit.*

52 Taylor, D. (2012) 'John Terry Trial Vignettes', *Guardian*, 13 July.
    Accessed 18 May 2014. Available at: http://www.theguardian.com/
    football/2012/jul/13/john-terry-trial-vignettes

53 Taylor, D. (2012) 'John Terry is Cleared, but Football's Reputation
    Takes a Battering', *Guardian*, 13 July. Accessed 18 May 2014. Avail-
    able at: http://www.theguardian.com/football/2012/jul/13/john-
    terry-cleared-football-reputation

54 BBC Radio 4 (2012) *Today*, 14 December. With reference to the racist
    behaviour of fans, Ouseley also makes the extraordinary comment,
    'if necessary, games should be stopped and sections of the crowd
    should be shown the door'. Let's hope it's never that easy to halt a
    game when your side is losing. See: Jones, D. (2012) 'Lord Ouseley:
    Football Games Should Be Stopped When Racism Occurs', *Goal*, 14
    December. Accessed 16 June 2014. Available at: http://www.goal.
    com/en/news/9/england/2012/12/14/3602177/lord-ouseley-
    football-games-should-be-stopped-when-racism

55 Patterson, N. (2012) 'T-Shirt Protests Should Provide Wake-Up Call
    for the FA & Friends', *FootballSpeak*, 24 October. Accessed 18 May
    2014. Available at: http://footballspeak.com/post/2012/10/24/T-
    Shirt-Protest.aspx

56 Mann, B. (2012) 'Clattenburg is Cleared of Racial Abuse and Urged

to Sue Chelsea', *The Week*, 23 November. Accessed 18 May 2014. http://www.theweek.co.uk/football/racism-sport/50235/clattenburg-cleared-racial-abuse-and-urged-sue-chelsea

57   Arrowsmith, R. (2012) '"Ill-Informed and Unhelpful": FA Hit Back at Criticisms Over Clattenburg Racism Case', *Daily Mirror*, 14 November. Accessed 18 May 2014. Available at: http://www.mirror.co.uk/sport/football/news/fa-hit-back-at-society-of-black-1435081

58   *Ibid.*

59   *SkyNews.com* (2012) 'FA Denies "Racist" Claim', *SkyNews.com*, 15 November. Accessed 22 May 2014. Available at: http://news.sky.com/story/1011571/fa-denies-racist-claim

60   Doyle, J. (2012) 'Kick it Out "Reassured" by FA's Clattenburg Investigation', *Goal*, 22 November. Accessed 18 May 2014. Available at: http://www.goal.com/en-ie/news/3941/england/2012/11/22/3548623/kick-it-out-reassured-by-fas-clattenburg-investigation

61   BBC Sport (2012) 'Peter Herbert "Ill-Advised" Says PFA's Clarke Carlisle', *BBC Sport*, 15 November. Accessed 21 May 2014. Available at: http://www.bbc.co.uk/sport/0/football/20337659

62   *Metro* (2012) 'David James: Racism in Football is an Agenda-Serving Myth', *Metro*, 11 October. Accessed 21 May 2014. Available at: http://metro.co.uk/2012/10/11/david-james-racism-in-football-is-an-agenda-serving-myth-598451/

63   Samuel, M. (2012) 'Football Is Not a Rancid Cess-pit of Racism', *Daily Mail*, 7 November. Accessed 18 May 2014. Available at: http://www.dailymail.co.uk/sport/article-2228993/Football-rancid-cesspit-racism-Martin-Samuel.html

64   Drayton, J. (2013) 'Anti-Racism Campaigner Elliot Resigns After his N-Word Rant at Rufus', *Daily Mail*, 23 February. Accessed 18 May 2014. Available at: http://www.dailymail.co.uk/sport/football/article-2283318/Paul-Elliott-resigns-FA-racism-row-Richard-Rufus.html

65   Waiton, S. (2012) 'Punters Paying the Penalty for Racism Storm', *The Scotsman*, 11 February. Accessed 18 May 2014. Available at: http://www.scotsman.com/news/stuart-waiton-punters-paying-the-penalty-for-racism-storm-1-2111122

66   Riach, J. (2013) 'Reginald D Hunter's Comedy Set at PFA Awards was "Huge Mistake"', *Guardian*, 29 April. Accessed 17 May 2014. Available at: http://www.theguardian.com/football/2013/apr/29/clarke-carlisle-reginald-hunter-pfa-awards

67   Samuel, M. (2012) *Op. cit.*

68   John Barnes interviewed on BBC Radio 4 *Today* programme, 13 February 2012.

69   Clarke Carlisle on BBC 1's *Question Time*, 1 March 2012.

70   You can listen to this clip from Eddie Nestor's *Drivetime* show here: http://m.youtube.com/watch?feature=share&v=1FUlTey0cnQ

Conclusion

On all matters concerning racism and fighting racism, the early part of my adult life was less confusing. Having grown up in small-town England in the 1960s and 70s, my lasting impression was that the world around me simply accepted racism — it was an everyday prejudice, something to laugh about while watching TV sit-coms. The menace of racism was largely ignored; although not completely ignored by me.

My shake of the DNA dice had given me a distinctly Asian-looking complexion. This was especially so as a child — I had jet black hair and skin just one degree too dark to ever convince anyone I was white. To this day, blue-eyed family members look at me and muse over what distant nuance of family history might explain such an anomaly. But, from 1973 (then aged 12) I was the nearest thing anyone had to a 'Paki' at the town's sprawling comprehensive. My PE teacher nicknamed me 'the coon'. This was a green light for kids to call me a lot of names — but mostly friendly ones like 'curry muncher' and 'Bombay Charlie'.

There were a lot of army kids who bussed in from the base nearby. A few, older than me, were originally from London. They took their racism far more seriously and regularly followed me around the school chanting 'nik nak grab a pak kick him in the head, all Pakistanis are better off dead'. I was never physically attacked; but in between shouting at them that I was, in fact, not a Pakistani, I like to think that I spared a thought for the real Asians who, I guessed, were somewhere up the road in London on the receiving end of venomous chants like that one.

They were. And they were getting stabbed and killed too. It wasn't until 1984 and my arrival in London to study at North East London Polytechnic that racism's grim reality hit home. And it hit me, then, that this was a reality egged along by politicians, magistrates and the police. Propelled from this experience into left-wing anti-racist campaigns, the path I had taken from my schooldays to the punky reggae party and Rock Against Racism gigs that followed, all conveniently timed to coincide with my teenage years, had something inevitable about it.

All the more strange, then, that on arrival in the twenty-first century, I was soon to find myself pitched against something calling itself 'anti-racism'. Many saw these new official, state-sponsored campaigns dedicated to eliminating racism 'in all its forms' as a victory. And indeed, had I been in a coma for the past 15 years, it might have seemed that I had woken up in an anti-racist utopia. Britain today bears no comparison with the predictable, everyday and often violent racism of the 1970s and 80s. Today, it is the *rarity* of discrimination, prejudice and violence that makes aberrant occurrences feel so shocking.

But it wasn't the new top-down official anti-racism that had suddenly beaten the menace back. Racism had already ceased to serve any function for the political elite. A new, confident diversity was bubbling up and the prejudices of the post-war generation now sounded, manifestly, like those of yesterday's world. As the twentieth century entered its final decades, the pendulum had swung to new forms of governance, laced with elite fears of race relations falling apart, and dedicated to the careful management of diversity. In other words, the flashing green light—that tacit nod of state approval toward everyday racism—had been switched off.

That is all great news. But how can we account for this reality gap, between a modern, diverse, increasingly race-indifferent Britain and an anti-racism obsessed with racial etiquette, identity and hurt feelings? In this book, I have tried to suggest that we peel away the labels of racism and anti-racism and look at what is really going on here.

The endless drives to expose 'diseased' speech and behaviour and the thoughts that give rise to it is, I contend, not motivated by a huge problem of racism, and nor will it do anything to counter the prejudices that do exist. Rather, the language of anti-racism has been co-opted by political and cultural elites, as a way to regulate spontaneous interaction and everyday behaviour. The result of this, as I have indicated, is to inflame sensitivities towards difference, and create resentments where none previously existed.

A movement that maps its prejudices over what constitutes racism *onto children* is especially worthy of our scepticism. By treating children as nasty little adults, whose playground behaviour should be treated with the assumptions and sanctions that we might use against die-hard racist adults, the very definition of 'children' and 'childhood' is grotesquely misunderstood. Moreover, the attempt to censure and correct children, to inculcate *goodthinking* and encourage racialised identities, cramps their ability to develop into independent, free-thinking grown-ups who can form their own opinions on questions of social injustice.

The soft tyranny of today's anti-racism lies in its intolerant demand that we all conform to a rigid set of cosmopolitan diversity rules. Its maxim is best summed up as 'intolerance will not be tolerated', the policy coda for which is 'zero tolerance'. In everyday public discourse the typical refrain is, 'but you can't say *that!*' Increasingly, though, we have already judiciously chosen not to say it. This, in my view, is the biggest problem of all.

Any social embargo that places a check on our public expressions and our private thoughts stifles the opportunity to speak, listen and make our own judgments. Such routine self-censorship will mean that all those attitudes and forms of expression, be they intolerant, hateful or merely heretical, that do not fit with the orthodoxy promoted by the political and media elite become cast as blasphemous and forced underground.

Regardless of whether these forms of expressions include ideas, images or words that you or I find vile or offensive — and the chances are they will — this cannot be a good thing. Bad ideas need to be out in the open, contested and fully exposed to scrutiny and argument. Otherwise we will never get the measure of what these bad ideas are, or the satisfaction of seeing them defeated.

Paradoxically, the suppression of what we or our rulers might term 'hate speech' creates perverse effects. Like children told not to behave childishly, adults treated like children become prompted to let their id go crazy and burst into untrammelled invective. As such, these moments — currently so frequently the preserve of Twitter — become perfect blips on the official anti-racist radar. They become seen as the most vivid of exposures, the tip of society's iceberg of unwitting racism, rather than the isolated, ill-thought-out, often frankly mad or drunken outbursts that they often are.

In its teacher training materials, the anti-racism education charity Show Racism the Red Card includes a diagram described as 'The Pyramid of Hate'.[1] Variations of this diagram flash up as powerpoint slides during public sector diversity training sessions with predictable regularity.[2] At the base of the pyramid we see 'prejudiced attitudes'; above that 'acts of prejudice' (described as 'name calling', 'telling belittling jokes'); above that, 'discrimination' (employment, housing, education); then 'violence'; and right at the top, 'genocide'.[3]

The diagram is designed to illustrate an inevitable escalating sequence. Without anti-racist intervention to challenge, as Ealing Hate Crime Support Project puts it, the 'more subtle acts of bias' and prevent the creation of 'an environment in which hatred and discrimination can flourish', each level will act as a conveyor-belt to the next.[4] Within this paranoid worldview, anti-racist policy assumes a vital role as the only way of protecting us from the consequences of each other — not to mention ourselves. Rather than being capable of critical thought and

reflection and open to debate and discussion, people are conceived of as unable to do the right thing without official super-
vision and monitoring.

Our belief in escalating chain reactions of hate, or simply in
the intrinsic power of certain words, phrases, objects and
images to either incite or cause wounding offence, depends on
two factors. The first is whether we are prone to imagine that a
zombie racism stalks the land. To keep a critical eye out for new
forms of racism is one thing. But in the trigger-happy zombie-
hunt that characterises today's anti-racist mindset, we are wit-
nessing something far more at ease with waging war on the
racism of yesteryear. Unplugged from the forces that fed it, we
might imagine that this racism feasts on our 'unwitting'
thoughts. In fact, it is simply dead.

The second factor, linked to the first, concerns our view on
what it is to be human. In the messy world of human interaction, words are imagined to possess their own racist power
independently of who has said them. They become at once
flying bombs equipped with warheads of offence, as well as
incantations casting racist spells on impressionable minds. So
fragile and flawed are we assumed to be that words alone have
the power to unleash racist attitudes in the listener: which, in
turn, has the power to unleash a social chain reaction of racist
bullying, discriminatory laws, violence and genocide. So we
find ourselves sinking into the quicksand of an anti-racism of
endless slights.

We have to ask ourselves, do these caricatures of the
unwitting racist and the pious anti-racist have anything in
common with how we think about our friends, neighbours,
colleagues, children? Do they have anything in common with
how we see ourselves?

History is full of those moments where we find ourselves
inspired by people transcending their differences and demanding, not to be protected, but to stand up and be counted. When
we think about those moments, we can remind ourselves about
our hope for the future. To turn our back on that instinct and be
drawn into the divisive politics of ethnic difference is to be

enticed by a simplistic, black-and-white narrative of racism which gains its momentum, not from the present, but from the past.

So we have a choice. We can fear the nightmare vision of a society in which racism lurks unwittingly just under the surface, demanding that we think twice before we speak and that we watch out for any potentially offensive joke or comment made by the person sitting next to us. Or we can embrace the genuine diversity that is expressing itself in our offices, in our neighbourhoods and on the playgrounds of our primary schools — if only we can bring ourselves to accept that it exists.

Endnotes:

[1]   Show Racism the Red Card (2010) 'Guidance for Initial Teacher Trainers'. See: http://www.srtrc.org/uploaded/ITT%20ED%20 PACK.pdf. Accessed on 21 May 2014. Also see: http://www. theredcard.ie/teachers.php and www.theredcard.org/uploaded/ Pyramid%20of%20hate(1).doc

[2]   In most cases the ubiquitous 'Pyramid of Hate' diagram derives from 'Allport's Scale of Prejudice' devised by the American psychologist and advocate of 'semantic therapy' Gordan Allport in the 1950s. Allport argued for the regulation of speech as a way 'to liberate a person from ethnic or political prejudice'. Racist and anti-communist prejudice was of course rife in 1950s America and doubtless 'antilocution' played its part in reinforcing elite-sanctioned prejudices that would sometimes take a more severe form. Today the *Pyramid of Hate* is wrenched from any historical or political context and used to infer something inevitable about untrammelled human nature which anti-racist policy must ameliorate or suppress.

[3]   Also see: Ealing Hate Crime Support Project (2010) 'The Links between Hate Crime, Discrimination and Prejudice', p19. Accessed on 21 May 2014. Available at: http://www.ealingnetwork.org.uk/ documents/guidance/ealing%20hate%20crime%20manual.pdf

[4]   Ealing Hate Crime Support Project (2010) *Op. cit.*, p19.

Postscript

Across the month of May 2014, as I was completing the manuscript for this book, the British press was dominated by stories concerning apparently shocking manifestations of racism. The month began with a revelation by the *Daily Mirror* that BBC *Top Gear* presenter Jeremy Clarkson had mumbled the 'n-word' in previously never-seen footage showing him recite the old rhyme 'Eeny, meeny, miny, mo...'.[1] The Labour MP Harriet Harman tweeted, 'Anybody who uses the n-word in public or private in whatever context has no place in the British Broadcasting Corporation'.[2]

As the furore over whether Clarkson should be sacked played out, the media returned again and again to the accusation of racism within the United Kingdom Independence Party (Ukip) and its supporters. This was, by now, a familiar theme. In April a Ukip candidate had tweeted that the comedian Lenny Henry should emigrate to 'a black country' (the candidate was forced to resign).[3] By the end of May the popularity enjoyed by Ukip at the European elections triggered intense discussion over the perceived problem of a growing popular racism. Explanations centred on an increase in anti-immigration sentiment amongst the British public, to which Ukip was allegedly fast becoming the beneficiary. As if to prove that straightforward racism lay at the heart of this phenomenon, the *Guardian*'s front page 'exclusive' for 27 May 2014, just days after Ukip's electoral success, ran with the headline 'Rising Tide of Race Prejudice Across Britain'.[4]

The *Guardian* had been granted access to an early release of data from the forthcoming British Social Attitudes (BSA) survey conducted by the social research agency NatCen. The survey appeared to show that levels of racial prejudice had increased since the beginning of the century, returning to the levels of 30 years ago. Interpreting the data, journalists Hugh Muir and Matthew Taylor asserted: 'the proportion of Britons who admit to being racially prejudiced has risen since the start of the millennium, raising concerns that growing hostility to immigrants and widespread Islamophobia are setting community relations back 20 years.'[5]

Accompanying this statement was a graph of the BSA data showing the percentage of those respondents who had admitted harbouring some level of racial prejudice. Curiously, it lumped together 'very prejudiced' and 'a little prejudiced' into a single percentage. But even more curious was how the graph itself showed that in 1983, when the survey began, 36 percent said they had 'some level of prejudice' and in the most recent year — 2013 — the figure is 30 percent. Along the way the graph zig-zags up and down. True, at the turning of the millennium the figure was at a low of 25 percent, but this was also the case in 2012 (at 26 percent). Insofar as self-reported 'racial prejudice' tells us anything, you would have to say the trend here is *downward*. Yet: 'The overall trend is upward', asserted Hugh Muir in a follow-on article a few days later, titled 'The Prejudice Pandemic Parting the UK'.[6]

In an age marked by unprecedented levels of ethnic harmony *and*, paradoxically, an ever-increasing official anti-racism intent on purging us of our 'unwitting' racism, the BSA data is not, given the vogue for *mea culpa*, all that surprising. It was left to BBC Radio 4's *More or Less* programme quietly to admonish the *Guardian*'s misinterpretation of the BSA data but also to make the point, 'what people mean when they admit racial prejudice now may be a very different thing than what they meant 30 years ago'.[7] For anti-racist campaigners, however, the *Guardian*'s interpretation of the data had said all that needed to be said. 'This nails the lie that the problem of racism has been overcome in Britain or that somehow when Jeremy Clarkson said the things he did it is some sort of anomaly that does not tap into a wider problem', claimed Omar Khan, acting director of the Runnymede Trust.[8]

The predilection to assume that the problem lies with a racist public confirms this book's analysis, that important questions are evaded when today's society is viewed through the lens of the racism of the past. Instead of crying *'That's racist!'*, anti-racists would do better to ask why it is that, in our public life, critical faculties evaporate the moment evidence of racism is imagined. As just a few commentators have argued, far from being a racism-ridden blob, the public are increasingly aware of the prejudice *directed at them* by the political elite.[9]

Polls showed the vast majority were against Clarkson being sacked, not because of any fondness for the n-word (or indeed Clarkson) but because they were free to apply common sense. They could plainly see that mumbling a rhyme in a never-broadcast out-take from *Top Gear* is not the same as shouting the n-word at a black person in the street.

Similarly, while Ukip may fixate on border controls, its victory in the European and local elections is better explained by the detachment and disdain of the political elite than by easily-pigeonholed racist attitudes. One commentator describes Ukip's support as rooted in 'a profound feeling of cultural insecurity', in being continually told to 'mind their language, police their thoughts, suppress their views, respect all cultures, hide their traditions, be ashamed of their national histories, never wave their national flags, and so on'.[10] Another comment-ator describes Ukip as 'political anti-matter… a cipher for all the anger and anxiety that voters feel'.[11]

Glib anti-racist explanations fail to understand phenomena such as the rise of Ukip. To do so, we have to adopt an open mind and engage with the serious political problems of the present.

Endnotes:

1   Collins, D. (2014) 'Jeremy Clarkson N-Word Shame: Top Gear Presenter Caught on Camera Using Racist Rhyme'.

2   Press Association (2014) 'Harman Urges BBC to Sack Clarkson', *MSN News,* 2 May. Accessed 12 June 2014. Available at: http://news.uk.msn.com/uk/harman-urges-bbc-to-sack-clarkson

3   Gander, K. (2014) 'Ukip Council Candidate William Henwood Resigns as Party Member Over Lenny Henry Racism Row', *Independent,* 29 April. Accessed 12 June 2014. Available at: http://www.independent.co.uk/news/uk/home-news/ukip-council-candidate-william-henwood-resigns-as-party-member-after-lenny-henry-racism-row-9303738.html

4   Taylor, M., and Muir, H. (2014) 'Racism on the Rise in Britain', *Guardian,* 27 May. Accessed 12 June 2014. Available at: http://www.theguardian.com/uk-news/2014/may/27/-sp-racism-on-rise-in-britain

5   *Ibid.*

6   Muir, H. (2014) 'The Prejudice Pandemic Parting the UK', *Guardian,* 1 June 2014. Accessed 12 June 2014. Available at: http://www.theguardian.com/uk-news/2014/jun/01/britains-prejudice-pandemic-race-religion-pollyanna-henny-penny?commentpage=1

7   *More or Less?* 'A Racist Trend?', BBC Radio Four, 01 June 2014. Accessed 12 June 2014. Available at: http://www.bbc.co.uk/programmes/p0202vm5. *The Economist* was also unequivocal in its shredding of the *Guardian*'s interpretation of the BSA data. See: *The Economist* (2014) 'Pride and Prejudice: Britain is Becoming Less Racist Not More', 31 May. Accessed 14 June 2014. Available at: http://www.economist.com/news/britain/21603056-britain-becoming-less-racist-not-more-pride-and-prejudice

8   Taylor, M., and Muir, H. (2014) *Op. cit.*

9   Hume, M. (2014) 'Clarkson: The C-Word that Counts is "Context"', *Spiked,* 6 May. Accessed 12 June 2014. Available at: http://www.spiked-online.com/freespeechnow/fsn_article/clarkson-the-c-word-that-counts-is-context#.U5GL39JdXfI

10   O'Neill, B. (2014) 'Nigel Farage and the Fury of the Elites', *Spiked,* 21 May. Accessed 12 June 2014. Available at: http://www.spiked-online.com/newsite/article/nigel-farage-and-the-fury-of-the-elites/15045#.U42jl9JdXfI

11   Sylvester, R. (2014) 'Power Would Annihilate the People's Army', *Times,* 27 May. Accessed 12 June 2014. Available at: http://www.thetimes.co.uk/tto/opinion/columnists/article4100847.ece

Bibliography

Barry, Brian. (2001) *Culture & Equality*. Cambridge: Polity Press.

Cantle, Ted. (2001) *Community Cohesion: A Report of the Independent Review Team Chaired by Ted Cantle*. London: Home Office.

Dennis, Norman, Erdos, George, and Al-Shahi, Ahmed. (2000) *Racist Murder and Pressure Group Politics: The Macpherson Report and the Police*. London: Civitas.

Furedi, Frank. (2011) *On Tolerance: A Defence of Moral Independence*. London: Continuum.

Heartfield, James. (2002) *The 'Death of the Subject' Explained*. Sheffield: Hallam Press.

Hewitt, Roger. (2005) *White Backlash and the Politics of Multiculturalism*. Cambridge: Cambridge University Press.

Kyriakides, Christopher, and Torres, Rodolfo. (2012) *Race Defaced: Paradigms of Pessimism, Politics of Possibility*. Stanford: Stanford University Press.

Lasch-Quinn, Elisabeth. (2001) *Race Experts: How Racial Etiquette, Sensitivity Training, and New Age Therapy Hijacked the Civil Rights Movement*. New York: Norton.

Malik, Kenan. (2008) *Strange Fruit: Why Both Sides Are Wrong in the Race Debate*. London: Oneworld Publications.

Malik, Kenan. (2009) *From Fatwa to Jihad: The Rushdie Affair and Its Legacy*. London: Atlantic Books.

Orwell, George. (1949) *Nineteen Eighty-Four*. London: Twentieth Century Classics.

Sewell, Tony. (2009) *Generating Genius: Black Boys in Love, Ritual and Schooling*. Stoke-on-Trent: Trentham Books.

Tompson, Keith. (1988) *Under Siege: Racial Violence in Britain Today*. London: Penguin Books.

Waiton, Stuart. (2012) *Snobs' Law: Criminalising Football Fans in an Age of Intolerance*. Take a Liberty (Scotland).

Index

The Author

Adrian Hart is a teacher turned film-maker who now writes exclusively about anti-racism, race and the official regulation of hate speech. His first publication *The Myth of Racist Kids* (The Manifesto Club, 2009) was quickly followed by *Leave Those Kids Alone* (2010) and numerous articles for the online current affairs magazine *spiked*. Hart lived, studied and worked in London for twenty years before moving to Brighton in 2003. He participated in late 1980s/early 1990s East London anti-racism campaigns prior to living, briefly, in Los Angeles. From 1997 his film-making prioritised the participation of children and for 10 years he worked on video projects in schools collaborating with various London arts organisations. Films include *Safe* (2002 winner of LWTs *Whose London?* competition) and *Only Human* (made in 2006 as an educational resource for Essex primary schools). You can follow Adrian Hart's writing or contact him via adrianhart.com.